GW00913552

Trading secrets

FT Prentice Hall
FINANCIAL TIMES

In an increasingly competitive world, we believe it's quality of thinking that gives you the edge – an idea that opens new doors, a technique that solves a problem, or an insight that simply makes sense of it all. The more you know, the smarter and faster you can go.

That's why we work with the best minds in business and finance to bring cutting-edge thinking and best learning practice to a global market.

Under a range of leading imprints, including *Financial Times Prentice Hall*, we create world-class print publications and electronic products bringing our readers knowledge, skills and understanding, which can be applied whether studying or at work.

To find out more about Pearson Education publications, or tell us about the books you'd like to find, you can visit us at **www.pearsoned.co.uk**

PEARSON
Education

Trading secrets

20 hard and fast rules to help you beat
the stock market

Simon Thompson

 Prentice Hall
FINANCIAL TIMES

An imprint of Pearson Education

Harlow, England • London • New York • Boston • San Francisco • Toronto • Sydney • Singapore • Hong Kong
Tokyo • Seoul • Taipei • New Delhi • Cape Town • Madrid • Mexico City • Amsterdam • Munich • Paris • Milan

PEARSON EDUCATION LIMITED

Edinburgh Gate
Harlow CM20 2JE
Tel: +44 (0)1279 623623
Fax: +44 (0)1279 431059
Website: www.pearsoned.co.uk

First published in Great Britain in 2009

© Simon Thompson 2009

The right of Simon Thompson to be identified as author of this work has been asserted
by him in accordance with the Copyright, Designs and Patents Act 1988.

ISBN: 978-0-273-72209-0

British Library Cataloguing-in-Publication Data
A catalogue record for this book is available from the British Library

Library of Congress Cataloging-in-Publication Data
A catalog record for this book is available from the Library of Congress

All rights reserved. No part of this publication may be reproduced, stored in a retrieval
system, or transmitted in any form or by any means, electronic, mechanical, photocopying,
recording or otherwise, without either the prior written permission of the publisher or a
licence permitting restricted copying in the United Kingdom issued by the Copyright
Licensing Agency Ltd, Saffron House, 6–10 Kirby Street, London EC1N 8TS. This book may
not be lent, resold, hired out or otherwise disposed of by way of trade in any form of binding
or cover other than that in which it is published, without the prior consent of the Publishers.

10 9 8 7 6 5 4 3 2 1
12 11 10 09 08

Typeset in 9/13pt Stone Serif by 30
Printed and bound in Great Britain by Ashford Colour Press Ltd, Gosport, Hants

The publisher's policy is to use paper manufactured from sustainable forests.

To my dearest wife, Wendy – your wonderful support over the years has made this book possible.

Contents

Author's acknowledgements

I would like to extend a warm thank you to stock market historian David Schwartz for all his help and assistance in writing this book. I am also very grateful to *Investors Chronicle* magazine and the London Stock Exchange for use of their archives. In particular, I would thank Chris Dillow of *Investors Chronicle* who has, over the years, provided me with some thought-provoking and intellectual stimulus that has certainly helped me uncover several of the trading secrets included in this book.

My thanks also to James Stack, President of Stack Financial Management and editor of *InvesTech Market Analyst* and *Portfolio Strategy*; John Hussman, President of Hussman Investment Trust; and Hans Wagner of Tradingmarketsonline.com, who all kindly allowed me to use some of their research in the book.

I am also indebted to several academics who, without fail, have offered me great support. For their assistance and use of their research in the area of seasonal investing and seasonal affective disorder in the stock market, I single out Mark Kamstra of the Schulich School of Business, York University, Lisa Kramer of the Joseph L. Rotman School of Management, University of Toronto, and Maurice Levi of the Saunder School of Business, University of Colombia.

For providing me with his research into the US presidential cycle, I owe a big thank you to Marshall Nickles of California's Pepperdine University's Graziadio School of Business and Management. For allowing me access to their findings on the January effect on the stock market, I am very grateful to John McConnell and Michael Cooper of the Krannert Graduate School of Management, Purdue University; Alexai Ovtchinnikov of the Vanderbilt Owen Graduate School of Management, Vanderbilt University; and Martin Bohl and Christian Salm of Westfalische Wilhelms-University.

I would like to thank both Laura Frieder of Krannert Graduate School of Management, Purdue University, and Avanidhar Subrahmanyam of the Anderson School of Management, University of California, whose work in the area of non-secular returns in the US stock market around religious days provided a firm basis for my work.

I would also extend my gratitude to Jay Dahya of the Zicklin School of Business, City University of New York, and Brian Mase of Brunel University for their research in the area of FTSE 100 constituents changes. My thanks also to Brian Lucey of Trinity College, Dublin, for his work on the Friday 13th effect and Glen Arnold and Rose Baker of Salford Business School for their research on return reversals in UK shares.

I am very grateful to Guy Kaplanski of Bar-Ilan University, Israel, and Haim Levy of the Hebrew University of Jersusalem for allowing me to use their academic paper on the FIFA World Cup effect on the US stock market. I would also like to extend my gratitude to Alex Edmans of the Wharton School, University of Pennsylvania, Diego Garcia of the University of North Carolina at Chapel Hill and Oyvind Norli of the Norwegian School of Management, who allowed me to use their research in the field of sports sentiment and stock returns.

The charts and financial data in this book would not have been provided in such detail without the great assistance of Thomson Reuters, the London Stock Exchange, Investors Intelligence and the Chicago Board Options Exchange – I am greatly indebted to you all.

Publisher's acknowledgements

We are grateful to the following for permission to reproduce copyright material:

Figures 1.1 and 1.2 from http://www.cboe.com/micro/vix/pricecharts.aspx; Figure 1.3 from Market Intervals Go Negative, 30 July 2007, http://www. hussmanfunds.com/wmc/wmc070730.htm. Reprinted by permission of Hussman Funds (www.hussmanfunds.com); Table 2.1 and Tables 7.2, 7.3 and 7.4 from Marshall D. Nickles, EdD, 'Presidential Elections and Stock Market Cycles,' 2004, *Graziadio Business Report*, Pepperdine University, http://gbr.pepperdine.edu/043/stocks.html; Figure 2.1 and Figure 12.1 from www.investorsintelligence.com; Tables 2.2 and 2.3 from Bearing up, *Investors Chronicle*, 15 March 2008 © Financial Times; Tables 4.1, 4.2, 5.2, 5.3, 13.1, 13.2, 15.3–15.6 and 20.1–20.4 from Thomson Datastream, © Thomson Reuters; Table 5.4 and Figure 5.1 and Graph 5 from Chris Dillow, Do sectors overreact? *Investors Chronicle*, 14 November 2007 © Financial Times; Table 6.3 from Trading Online Markets LLC, Hans E. Wagner, 24 September 2007; Figure 6.1 from Must stocks rise following a cut in the Fed funds rate? March 2007, http://www.hussman.net/rsi/fedfundscut.htm. Reprinted by permission of Hussman Funds (www.hussmanfunds.com); Figure 8.1 from http://www.londonstockexchange.com/en-gb/pricesnews/education/interchange/Authors/davidschwartz/volatilityisabearmarketsignal.htm.

We are grateful to the following for permission to reproduce the following texts:

Extract Chapter 1 (p.5) from Market Intervals Go Negative, 30 July 2007, http://www.hussmanfunds.com/wmc/wmc070730.htm. Reprinted by permission of Hussman Funds (www.hussmanfunds.com); Extracts Chapter 6 (p. 67) Must stocks rise following a cut in the Fed funds rate? March 2007, http://www.hussman.net/rsi/fedfundscut.htm. Reprinted by permission of Hussman Funds (www.hussmanfunds.com).

In some instances we have been unable to trace the owners of copyright material, and we would appreciate any information that would enable us to do so.

About the author

Simon Thompson has been Companies Editor at *Investors Chronicle*, the UK's leading investment magazine for private investors, for eight years and has worked as a financial journalist for ten years with the Financial Times Group in London. He has a BSc degree in banking and international finance from the Cass Business School, City University, London.

Simon is also a regular speaker at seminars on equity market strategy, including events for the London Stock Exchange, investment bank Société Générale, the UK's biggest spread betting group, IG Index, and Selftrade, one of the UK's largest stockbrokers. He has proved a shrewd judge when it comes to market timing, correctly calling the top of the bull market in the UK on 25 June 2007 (Thompson, 2007b) and the top of the US bull market on 9 July 2007 (Thompson, 2007c). He also proved prescient with his prediction of a savage downturn in global equity markets at the start of 2008. The short index trades he advised in the first half of 2008 returned an average profit of 50 per cent (Thompson, 2008d).

Simon also has an outstanding record at stockpicking. Between 2004 and 2007, he gave 67 stock and index recommendations in his companies column in the *Investors Chronicle*, of which 90 per cent showed a profit and an average gain of 33 per cent (Thompson, 2007a). In 2005, Simon had a 100 per cent track record, with all 16 of his recommendations in his column that year recording a profit (Thompson, 2005b).

List of figures and tables

Figures

Tables

Preface

When I decided to write *Trading Secrets*, I had a very clear objective: to produce a book that encapsulated the best stock market trading ideas that I have discovered during my 20 years of following financial markets. I wanted the book to be both educational and practical, with the intention that both experienced private investors as well as those with little or no knowledge of the stock market could benefit and profit from these strategies. In fact, *Trading Secrets* has turned out to contain all the trading strategies that I wish I had known about when I started following the stock market during the 1980s bull market. It has taken me two decades to get this far, so the book will give all investors a head start, and a profitable one at that, in their investing careers.

Each chapter is broken down into sections, laid out in an easy-to-understand format. A description is given of the stock market trend or apparent anomaly that enables shrewd investors in the know to consistently make money. Knowing that a trend or anomaly exists is one thing, but more important is understanding why it occurs, so I have included a section entitled 'Reasons for the phenomenon' in each of the chapters before outlining the best trading strategy to use to profit from those trends and anomalies.

The book includes trading strategies that can be used by investors in either the short or long term, the economic and stock market cycle and are specific to the US and UK stock markets. This makes *Trading Secrets* unique as it offers clear-cut strategies for all investors to follow, with each one being easy to implement. Most important of all, these *Trading Secrets* have proved very profitable.

Introduction

The great advantage of studying the stock market, and trends in particular, is that we can quickly identify certain patterns forming that bear a scary resemblance to ones from the past. History may not repeat itself in exactly the same way, but in some cases it gets eerily close and that's what *Trading Secrets* is all about. It reveals the trends and apparent stock market anomalies that have stood the test of time and, for those in the know, provide a regular source of profitable trading opportunities.

The bear market of 2007 and 2008 may have savaged the share portfolios of many investors, but not all. For instance, when I called the bull market top in the US stock market on 9 July 2007 (Thompson, 2007c) a few days before the Dow Jones Industrial Average hit its record high of 14022 that summer, I knew certain things that very few investors were aware of. However, if they had been, they would have joined me in bolting for the door.

First, the Coppock curve was giving a major warning signal of a market top – one that it had only given six times in the past eight years. Note that this indicator has a great record of calling both market tops and bear market lows. Second, the US stock market had not once fallen by 10 per cent during the bull market that had started in October 2002. This was the second longest period since 1921 that the market had risen without suffering a correction of at least 10 per cent. Third, it may be a little-known fact, but not a single bull market in the US that started in the second year of the decade has managed to run past the seventh year. Add to this other key indicators that were sending out distress signals and the writing was on the wall that the 2002–2007 bull market was running out of steam in July 2007. Fifteen months later, the Dow had fallen by 40 per cent. In Chapter 1, Bull market tops, I reveal my 15 optimum signals for calling bull market tops in both the US and UK.

There are also some fantastic indicators for timing major market lows, including the McClellan index, Advisor Sentiment Survey readings, divergence of share prices from their long-term averages and over 100 years of stock market history. For example, I knew in late 2007 that the UK bear market would not be over until share prices had dropped by at least 25 per cent. This was great news because every time stocks rallied, the correct and very profitable trading strategy was to sell once the rallies ran out of steam. In Chapter 2, Bear market bottoms, I reveal the ten indicators you can use to profit from bear markets.

It certainly pays to keep a close watch on the political calendar. In Chapter 7, US presidential cycle, I outline two trading strategies that have a 100 per cent track record for rewarding investors generously over the past 40 years on both sides of the Atlantic. The Chancellor's Budget in March should not be ignored either as there are regularly great trading opportunities at that time of the year, but only if you know how to profit from them. Chapter 17, Budgeting for profit, reveals those particular *trading secrets*.

Don't turn a blind eye to what the US central bank, the Federal Reserve, is up to. In Chapter 6, Federal Reserve's rate-cutting cycles, I outline a trading strategy that has a 100 per cent track record over the past seven rate-cutting cycles and has delivered an average annual return of 17.5 per cent on the S&P 500 Index.

Friday the 13th may be unlucky for some, but not if you are privy to one of the best kept trading secrets in the stock market. In Chapter 14, Days like these, I show how investors are far from superstitious on these days of the year. In fact, they are likely to be in buoyant mood. Don't forget to make a note on your calendar of the four days of the year when triple witching takes place. It may sound like something that has more in common with Hallowe'en than the financial markets, but investors ignore this important date at their peril as it has a significant impact on how equity markets behave at certain points in the year (see Chapter 20 on triple witching).

In a similar vein, it's worth making an unmissable note in your diary of when certain religious holidays and sporting events take place. Most investors probably don't realise that they can have an impact on the stock market, but they certainly do. Chapters 11, Religious holidays, and 18, Sporting chance, reveal the best trading strategies to profit from these days on the calendar.

It's also worth monitoring changes to the constituents of the FTSE 100 as this has proved a fruitful hunting ground for making gains from the poor performers in the index in the past (see Chapter 13, Playing footsie), and don't ignore shares that have performed atrociously for years on end as they have a habit of suddenly springing into life. There is a very good reason for these sudden price moves. In Chapters 15, S&P 500 dog effect, and 16, Dogs of the FTSE All-Share Index, I outline two short-term trading strategies that have delivered very healthy returns to investors in the know over the years.

Most of all, don't forget your history books. These have proved a treasure trove of profitable but little-known *trading secrets*, as I show in Chapter 19 (History lessons) as well as Chapters 8 (Summertime blues) and 9 (Predictive powers). So, armed with *Trading Secrets'* top strategies, investing can be not only enjoyable but also be very profitable.

Simon Thompson

Bull market tops

S tock markets are pretty unforgiving and it pays to know the warning signs for when they will turn well in advance of when they actually do. That is the problem for most investors as jumping off the up escalator is one of the hardest things to do.

> **when a bull market tops out, stocks retrace their gains in a far more linear fashion on the way down than on the way up**

When a bull market tops out, the one thing to remember is that stocks retrace their gains in a far more linear fashion on the way down than they rise on the way up. This makes it even more important to know when to take your money off the table and bank profits, otherwise you could end up donating those hard-won gains made over the course of a bull run back to the market in double quick time.

> **the worry or greed factor of missing out on further potential stock gains will always impact our judgement**

The worry or greed factor of missing out on further potential stock gains will always impact our judgement at such times. Fortunately, there are 15 leading indicators that have stood the test of time to make the decision as to when to bank profits a much easier process.

US bull market tops

Trend 1: Equity inflows into mutual funds

A reliable sign of an impending market top is when there are very high levels of capital flows into stock mutual funds and equity exchange traded funds (ETFs). For example, in the months leading up to the US stock market peak in July 2007, equity fund inflows hit a record high of over $10 billion a week. This was the first major warning signal of the market nearing a top. It was a similar story in early 2000 when inflows to funds peaked out, too – a prelude to the market's bull run ending three months later.

This has been such a great indicator, for the simple fact that US retail investors will normally invest in mutual funds and ETFs as part of their long-term investment strategy and these payments will usually be taken from monthly salaries. However, spikes in these flows are more likely to be sentiment-driven, as investors become overly bullish and react to the bull market euphoria that has in the past marked the peak in stock prices.

❝ a reliable sign of an impending market top is when high levels of capital flows into stock mutual funds ❞

TrimTabs Investment Research is the only independent research service that publishes detailed daily coverage of US stock market liquidity, including mutual funds and ETFs (visit: **www.trimtabs.com**).

Trend 2: Volatility index

The volatility index – or VIX as it is known – measures the volatility of index options listed on the Chicago Board Options Exchange (CBOE). In effect, it can be considered a sentiment indicator or Wall Street's greed or fear gauge. Many traders use it to measure the degree of investor complacency or market fear.

❝ many traders use the volatility index to measure the degree of investor complacency or market fear ❞

In early 2007, the VIX hit a record low of around 10, indicating that investors piling into the US stock market were getting far too comfortable (see Figure 1.1). Note that the VIX, or level of market fear, was still at an historic low of around 15 when the market topped out in July 2007. The indicator was spot on, with the stock market plunging at the end of the month and the VIX doubling to over 30.

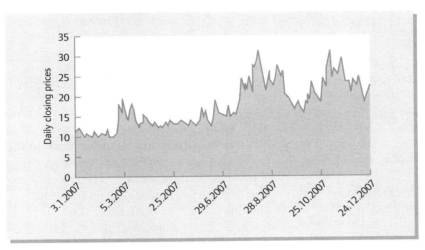

figure 1.1 CBOE volatility index and performance of S&P 500 Index in 2007
(3 January–31 December)   Sources: CBOE and Bloomberg

The experience in 2007 was not an isolated example either as low readings in the VIX in 1994, 1998 and 2000 all came a matter of months
before the stock market topped out (see Figure 1.2).

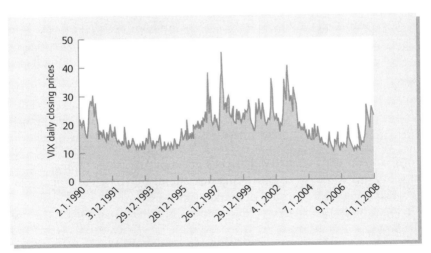

figure 1.2 CBOE volatility index since 1990 (2 January 1990–14 January 2008)

Sources: CBOE and Bloomberg

It is therefore worth keeping a close eye on the VIX, which can be monitored on the CBOE's website (at: **www.cboe.com**). Remember, extremely low levels of market volatility – VIX in the range 10–15 – indicates that investors are being far too complacent and, in the past, has corresponded with periods when the bull run in the stock market is close to peaking out.

Trend 3: Advancing/declining stocks

The advancing/declining (A/D) line is of great interest to investors calling bull market tops because it reveals how strongly based the advance in stock prices is. As the major US indices such as the Nasdaq Composite, Nasdaq 100 and S&P 500 are weighted according to the market capitalisations of the constituent companies, the A/D line tells us what is really happening below the surface.

> **" the advancing/declining line is of great interest to investors because it reveals how strongly based the advance in stock prices is "**

For instance, if the indices are rallying but the A/D line is diverging, then it indicates that the funds flowing into equity markets are starting to fade – hardly a bullish signal. To see how the A/D line works in practice consider the US market tops in both March 2000 and July 2007. At the end of the dot.com boom eight years ago, the Nasdaq was making record highs, but the number of stocks leading the advance was diminishing. In effect, a decreasing number of stocks was leading the advance so the rally was narrowing in terms of its participation. It is clearly unsustainable for the market to continue rallying if the share prices of an ever smaller number of companies are advancing.

Fast forward to the summer of 2007 and investors were in an equally bullish mood with the Dow Jones Industrial Average hitting a sequence of record highs leading up to a record peak of 14022 on 17 July. However, below the surface all was not well – something that was not lost on James Stack, President of Stack Financial Management and Editor of *InvesTech Market Analyst* and *InvesTech Portfolio Strategy* (at: **www.investech.com**).

Mr Stack noted at the time that declining stocks had outnumbered advancing stocks in no fewer than seven of the eight sessions when the index closed higher in the run-up to those record highs (Stack, 2007). Further, on Monday 16 July 2007, the index hit yet another record high, despite decliners in the index outnumbering risers in the ratio of 2:1. That has never happened once in the past eight decades and was clear confirmation of negative breadth divergence. It was also an ominous sign of the turbulent times to follow: the index slumped by 10 per cent within the next 23 trading days.

Moreover, history shows that major market tops have been regularly associated with divergence of the A/D line and the apparent bullish price activity. Ultimately, the lack of breadth in the rally reveals itself when the diminishing number of stocks driving the market higher can no longer make up for the decliners in the index.

> ❝ lack of breadth in a rally reveals itself when the diminishing number of stocks driving the market higher can no longer make up for the decliners ❞

The website **www.stockcharts.com** monitors the A/D line for the Nasdaq, New York Stock Exchange and Amex – the third-largest stock exchange by trading volume in the USA.

Trend 4: Coppock indicators

Edwin S. Coppock developed his Coppock guide or curve over 50 years ago and his indicator has a fantastic record for signalling the start of a new bull market (see Chapter 2). However, it can also be used to identify bull market tops. That is because Coppock is a momentum oscillator. It is based on the ten-month smoothing of the averaged 14-month and 11-month rate of change in the S&P 500, so will reverse direction when momentum in the stock market peaks out.

> ❝ when a double top occurs in the Coppock curve, without ... falling to zero between those peaks, 'it identifies a runaway market heading for disaster ❞

Mr Stack noted that, in the late 1960s, technician Don Hahn found when a double top occurs in the Coppock curve, without the curve falling to zero between those peaks, 'it identifies a bull market that hasn't experienced any normal, healthy washouts or corrections. That's a runaway market usually headed for disaster. This double top has occurred only six times in 80 years' (Stack, 2007).

John Hussman, President of Hussman Investment Trust (**www.hussmanfunds.net**) noted those six instances and the subsequent market losses were: October 1929, –86.2 per cent; May 1946, –28.8 per cent; February 1969, –36.1 per cent; January 1973, –48.2 per cent; September 1987, –33.5 per cent; and April 1998, a prelude to a 18 per cent market correction by October 1998. Interestingly, the subsequent recovery in the US stock market after October 1998 then produced a third 'shelf' in the Coppock curve in 2000. The market then lost nearly half of its value between 2000 and 2002 (Hussman, 2007).

True to form, the Coppock curve gave a second peak in the first half of 2007. This was an ominous sign as the US bull market rally from October 2002 to July 2007 had not been interrupted by a major correction of 10 per cent. By October 2008, the S&P 500 had fallen by 43 per cent from that 2007 record high.

So, the next time the market makes a double top in the Coppock curve without having had a correction (defined as a 10 per cent fall in the market) during its bull run, then this is a massive warning signal to start banking profits. The market would have to defy eight decades of history to continue its bull run without first suffering a major plunge. So far, it has never been able to achieve that.

Investors Chronicle (**www.investorschronicle.co.uk**) has been producing a Coppock index since 1963 for all the major financial markets, including the Dow Jones Industrial Average and Nasdaq 100, with free updates published online every month.

Trend 5: Bull markets, economic cycle and presidential cycle

Of interest in gauging market tops is the length of the bull market. Since the Great Depression, there have been 25 bull markets in the US, covering the period from 1932 to 2007.

It is worth noting that the last bull market started on 10 October 2002 and was 1827 days old when the Dow Jones Industrial Average hit its all-time peak of 14198 on 11 October 2007, making it the fourth longest in the past 75 years. However, only 8 of the 25 bull markets have lasted longer than 1000 days. So, the 2002–2007 bull run was quite exceptional in its longevity, especially as the average length of all the bull markets is 764 days, or, 25 months. Moreover, the average gain in the US stock market in all these 25 bull markets has been 78 per cent. The near doubling of share prices in the 2002–2007 bull market was well above average.

 ❝ not a single bull market that started in the second year of the decade has been able to run past the seventh ❞

Interestingly, there is one startling fact that has served investors well over the past seven decades: not a single bull market that started in the second year of the decade has been able to run past the seventh year of that decade. This is not some statistical quirk without a sound explanation. The reason is the US presidential cycle.

Bull market tops and the US presidential cycle

The US bull markets that started in October 2002, August 1982, June 1962, April 1942 and July 1932 have one thing in common: they all commenced between three and eight months before the start of pre-election year. As I will explain in Chapter 7, in the past five decades, the US stock market has not once failed to rise in pre-election year. This is mainly due to the monetary and fiscal stimulus the economy gets ahead of the US presidential elections, which investors react favourably to. As a result, the five bull markets above that started in the second year of the decade also got a helpful boost from the incumbent government administration from the start.

> **the convergence of the stock market cycle, the economic cycle and the US presidential cycle means bull markets starting in the second year of the decade are likely to be long runners**

As bull markets follow periods of economic slowdown or recession that had led to a prior bear market, most of these five bull markets above enjoyed a healthy tail wind from the ongoing economic recovery. So, the convergence of the peak-to-trough stock market cycle, the economic cycle and the four-year US presidential cycle means that bull markets starting in the second year of the decade are likely to be very long runners. In fact, the 1942, 1962 and 2002 bull runs were three of the four longest in history.

> **don't push your luck if a bull market that started in the second year of the decade is still running into the seventh**

Remember though not to push your luck if a bull market that started in the second year of the decade is still running into the seventh year of the decade. The odds are heavily stacked that a market top will occur before the end of the seventh year of the decade, as it did in October 2007. These long runners can only last so long before the equity markets finally get a reality check from the economic cycle.

Trend 6: Bull market corrections

Corrections of 10 per cent in stock prices are taken as part and parcel of bull markets. Indeed, the majority of bull markets in the past 80 years have lasted fewer than 200 days before a 10 per cent correction occurred (see Figure 1.3). These are generally seen as healthy events, taking the froth off stock prices and removing investor complacency before the next

❝ only 5 bull markets in the past 8 decades have run for more than 800 days without a correction of at least 10 per cent ❞

leg up of the bull market can begin. It's worth noting that only 5 bull markets in the past 8 decades have run for more than 800 days without a correction of at least 10 per cent. These are the exceptions as the majority of bull markets have struggled to last more than 200 days before a 10 per cent correction.

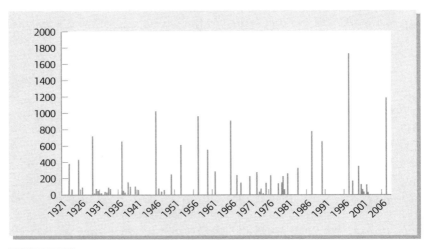

figure 1.3 Length of bull market without 10 per cent correction

Source: Hussman Funds

So, if the other bull market top signals are flashing red and the market has yet to correct by at least 10 per cent, it would pay to take notice.

Trend 7: US recession and bull market tops

Since 1945, there have been 11 recessions in the US, which have averaged about 10 months each. The longest lasted 16 months in 1981 and 1982 when the Federal Reserve, under Chairman Paul Volcker, raised interest rates to an eye-watering 20 per cent to battle soaring inflation. This can be painful for share prices.

This is not surprising as a downturn in economic activity is hardly good news for corporate profits, so it is only sensible that equity investors anticipate the onset of these slowdowns. In fact, every recession since 1945 has been preceded by falls in equity prices (see Table 1.1). In seven cases, these led to bear markets (a fall of 20 per cent or more), in three

> **66 every recession since 1945 has been preceded by falls in equity prices 99**

cases the stock market fell between 10 and 20 per cent and only once did investors get off lightly (5 to 10 per cent). On average, the sell-off in equity prices before and during recessions sent the S&P 500 Index tumbling down by over 25 per cent.

So, if a recession is on the way, then the odds are pretty short that a bull market top is not far away either. Fortunately, there is a fantastic leading indicator for the likelihood of a US recession.

Alan Reynolds, a senior fellow with the Cato Institute, notes that, in 1983, economist James Hamilton produced a thesis showing that 'all but one of the US recessions since the second world war have been preceded, typically with a lag of around nine months, by a dramatic increase in the price of crude petroleum' (Reynolds, 2008).

However, Professor Hamilton's findings were challenged a decade ago by academics Ben Bernanke (now the Chairman of the Federal Reserve), Mark Gertler and Mark Watson. They argued that it is difficult to isolate the effect of oil prices on recessions because 'a number of the most significant tightenings of US monetary policy have followed on the heels of major

table 1.1 US recessions and bear markets (1948–2007)

Recession start and end dates	Bear or bull market running at time
November 1948–October 1949	Bear: June 1948–June 1949
July 1953–May 1954	Bear: January 1953–September 1953
August 1957–April 1958	Bear: April 1956–October 1957
April 1960–February 1961	Bear: January 1960–October 1960
December 1969–November 1970	Bear: December 1968–May 1970
November 1973–March 1975	Bear: January 1973–October 1974
January 1980–July 1980	Bear: January 1978–April 1980
July 1981–November 1982	Bear: April 1981–August 1982
July 1990–March 1991	Bear: July 1990–October 1990
March 2001–September 2001	Bear: March 2000–October 2002

Source: Thomson Reuters Datastream

increases in the price of imported oil', adding that 'an important part of the effect of oil price shocks on the economy results not from the change in oil prices per se, but from the resulting tightening of monetary policy.'

Still, what can't be in dispute is that, during periods when both monetary policy is being tightened and the oil price has increased dramatically, the US has fallen into recession. Mr Reynolds found that, in the past four decades, there have been five occasions when the Federal Funds rate was increased above the ten-year US bond yield: 1969, 1973–1974, 1979–1981, 1989 and 2000. In every single case, the US economy was in recession a year later – in 1970, 1974–1975, 1980–1982, 1990 and 2001. What's more, each of these periods of monetary tightening followed significant rises in the oil price.

> ❝ during periods when both monetary policy is being tightened and the oil price has increased dramatically, the US has fallen into recession ❞

Fast forward to the summer of 2007 and the oil price had spiralled up from $50 a barrel in January of that year to $79 by August. The Federal rate was also above the ten-year bond yield and the yield curve had been inverted (with long-term yields below short-term yields) for several months – another leading indicator of a significant economic slowdown. This was a deadly combination and a warning sign to investors to bank their stock market gains. By October 2008, US stock prices had fallen a hefty 43 per cent.

The bottom line is that a rampant oil price, coupled with tighter US monetary policy and an inverted yield curve, is by far one of the best indicators of a US recession. As equity bull markets top out before the economy starts to slow, then it is a great leading indicator of a US bull market top and one that it is costly to ignore. Given the high correlation between the UK and US stock markets, and the fact that the UK and Europe are not immune to an economic slowdown in the US, this indicator works very well in predicting UK equity market tops, too.

> ❝ a rampant oil price, coupled with tighter US monetary policy and an inverted yield curve, is one of the best indicators of a US recession ❞

Trend 8: Sentiment indicators – put/call ratio

If the market in put and call options (which give the holder of the option the right to sell (in the case of puts) or buy (for calls) shares in a company at a predetermined price on a specific day) skews too much in one direction, it can be a great contrarian indicator (see Chapter 20 for an explanation of how the options market works).

At market tops, buyers of call options are most bullish, so the likelihood of a downside reversal in prices is greatest. By contrast, when investors become overly bearish so buy more puts than calls, an equity market rally may be on the horizon.

❝ at market tops, buyers of calls are most bullish, so the likelihood of a downside reversal in prices is greatest ❞

Investors can monitor activity in the options market through the Chicago Board Options Exchange (CBOE) total equity put/call ratio (daily data and charts available on **www.stockchart.com**). Every day, the CBOE adds together all of the call and put options traded on every stock and calculates the ratio of the volume of put option contracts to the volume of call option contracts.

On an average day, the put/call ratio is around 0.8, simply because investors are more likely, on average, to bet the market will rise, so are net buyers of calls. However, on days when the major indices rise strongly, the number of calls bought typically far outweighs the number of puts, so the put/call ratio may be very low. A drop below 0.6 indicates investor complacency and so is a bearish indicator. By contrast, on days of extreme market weakness, fear prevails among investors and the number of puts purchased can be far greater than calls – possibly reaching 1.1. As a result the put/call ratio has a decent record of identifying extreme market tops associated with euphoric buying as well as market bottoms associated with climatic selling.

Trend 9: Sentiment indicators – financial advisers surveys

Investment theory suggests that when too many market participants are overly bullish on prospects for the market, it is a sign that most investors have already invested. As a result of this over-optimism, there is a diminishing amount of cash waiting to enter the market, which is why this is an excellent contrarian indicator.

❝ when too many market participants are overly bullish on prospects for the market, this is a sign that most investors have already invested ❞

The Advisor Sentiment Survey, published by equity and bond research group, Investors Intelligence (**www.investorsintelligence.com**), is one of the longest-standing surveys of investors' levels of optimism. Past surveys have shown that market tops usually occur when over 60 per cent of those advisers questioned are bullish about the market. This is not an exact science, so advisers can be overly bullish for long periods before the market tops out, but it is an early warning signal nonetheless.

Trend 10: Sentiment indicators – US consumer confidence

It may seem obvious, but extreme readings in US consumer confidence are a great contrarian indicator of turning points in the equity markets. Overly bullish consumer optimism is regularly associated with market tops, while extreme pessimism is associated with market bottoms.

This indicator is quite easy to monitor as the Conference Board, one of the world's leading research organizations, produces its monthly 'Consumer confidence survey' based on a representative sample of 5000 US households. The results of the survey, including the all-important consumer confidence index (CCI), are available free online at **www.conference-board.org**.

❝ overly bullish consumer optimism is regularly associated with market tops, while extreme pessimism is associated with market bottoms ❞

As consumer spending is one of the bedrocks of the US economy, so is a significant factor in a country's well being, extreme CCI readings have been a useful contrarian indicator for the future stock market performance. For instance, in the run-up to the war in Iraq, the mood of US consumers was extremely downbeat in March 2003. However, this actually marked a major turning point in the equity bear market. By the same token, the 2000 bull market topped out on a wave of extreme consumer optimism that was clearly misplaced given the following economic slump and savage bear market.

To gauge how bullish or bearish US consumers are, it's worth noting that the CCI had a starting point of 100 in 1985, extremely bullish readings (and bearish for equity markets) are recorded above 115 and extreme bearish readings (and bullish for equity markets) are recorded when the index falls below 75. The 16-year low is 54.6 in October 1992 – a point from which the S&P 500 Index rallied 15 per cent in the following 14 months.

Interestingly, by October 2008, the CCI had fallen to an all time low of 38, a huge drop from the reading of 61 in September. Only time will tell if this extreme consumer gloom was overdone, but, if history is any guide this pointed to a short-term rally in the S&P 500 Index from its autumn lows at the very least.

Trend 11: IPO market and M&A activity

Bull markets tend to end on a wave of euphoria, with euphoric valuations, too. A sizzling hot IPO market is one very good indicator of an equity market that is getting overheated. For instance, a wave of technology flotations on Nasdaq at sky high valuations marked the top of the dot.com boom in 2000. It was a similar story in 2007, but this time a private equity debt-fuelled mergers and acquisitions (M&A) deal frenzy marked the top of the credit bubble that had driven equity market valuations to record levels.

> **a sizzling hot IPO market is one very good indicator of an equity market that is getting overheated ... a market top is not far away**

So next time a bull market has been running for some time and you read that M&A activity is hitting record levels and IPOs are running at a breakneck pace, this is more likely than not to be a warning sign that a market top is not far away.

Trend 12: Dow Jones Industrial Average/Nasdaq Composite Index ratio

The ratio of the Dow Jones Industrial Average to Nasdaq Composite indices is a real favourite and one that is so easy to monitor and understand. For the past two decades, the ratio between the two indices has been trading in the range 2.3 (at the time of the dot.com boom in late March 2000) to 6.9 (at the bottom of the bear market in early October 2002).

> **when the ratio is low this indicates investors are being more aggressive**

The great thing about the ratio is that it tells us how investors are thinking. When the ratio is low, then the technology-laden and more speculative Nasdaq index is outperforming the Dow Jones Industrial Average, which is full of blue chip corporations. This indicates that investors are being more aggressive and are willing to take on more risk than when the ratio is high.

By contrast, significant moves of the ratio towards the top of the 20-year range indicate that investors are being cautious and are weighting their investments towards the safer Dow Jones Industrial Average blue chip corporations. In effect, the ratio is a contrarian indicator and one that has served investors well over the years, calling the top of the US stock market in 2000 as well as giving a great 'buy' signal in the dark days of October 2002.

UK Bull market tops

Trend 13: US recessions and UK bear markets

In the past five decades there have been no fewer than six recessions in the US – possibly seven if the 2007/2008 economic slowdown gets any worse. Incredibly, the UK stock market has entered a bear market on every single occasion.

❝ there have been six recessions in the US, incredibly, the UK stock market has entered a bear market on every single occasion ❞

So, if there are worrying signs of a severe US economic slowdown, that is reason enough to sound the UK bull market alarm bells. Moreover, equity markets are forward-looking price mechanisms, so they discount potential bad news well in advance of the events taking place. Bearing this in mind, it would be sensible for bear markets to start before the US economy enters recession and trough out ahead of when the economic recovery begins.

❝ it would be sensible for bear markets to start before the US economy enters recession and trough out ahead of the economic recovery ❞

Research from investment magazine *Investors Chronicle* (Picarda, 2008), certainly backs up this theory: all bar one of the 11 post-war bear markets in the UK, that coincided with a US recession, started before the US entered recession and ended ahead of the subsequent economic recovery. On average, UK bear markets begin five months before the start of a US recession and finish four-and-a-half months before the recession ends. So, with this thought in mind, UK investors should be keeping a close eye on economic data from across the Atlantic as a leading indicator on when the 2007/2008 UK bear market, which started in June 2007, will end.

Trend 14: Bonds and commodities

Bonds

It is well worth paying close attention to other asset classes when looking for bull market tops. Generally, equities and bond prices both move up during bull markets, but the latter have historically changed direction first. This reflects the fact that interest rates tend to rise at the end of bull markets. Higher interest rates are a tool used by central banks to reduce the risk of economies overheating, as well as a way of keeping a lid on inflationary pressures. Not surprisingly, higher interest rates are bad news for bonds, the prices of which move in the opposite direction from the underlying movement in interest rates.

equities and bond prices both move up during bull markets, but the latter have historically changed direction first

The major UK equity market top in June 2007 certainly fits this pattern. Interest rates started to rise six months earlier, reflecting the Bank of England's tough stance on inflation, while bond prices had already peaked following a period when investors had driven down yields on this asset class to unsustainably low levels. This was not an isolated example either as bond market peaks in 1987, 1989, 1993 and 2000 all preceded significant equity market sell-offs in the UK.

Commodity prices

It's also worth keeping a close eye on commodity prices as these have a habit of rising at the end of equity bull markets. One of the drivers of commodity price inflation is a weak dollar. In fact, since 1995, the correlation between annual changes in the dollar's trade-weighted index and moves in commodity prices in the following 12 months has been 0.56 (Thomson Reuters Datastream). This alone explains almost a third of commodity price inflation. So, why does it happen?

The commonest explanation for the weak US dollar boosting commodity prices is that central banks in the Middle East and Asia peg their currencies to the dollar, printing money to support the weak dollar. In turn, some of this cash leaks out into higher demand for commodities. Again, the steep sell-off in the US dollar in the 12 months to May 2007 also coincided with a steep rise in commodity prices. The UK equity market peaked one month later.

Trend 15: Sector leadership

as a bull run matures it is usual for the oil, mining and other basic industries to lead the advance, while utilities and the financial sectors struggle

Industry leadership within the UK stock market also gives us clues as to potential market tops as different sectors tend to prosper at different stages of the equity market cycle. As a bull run matures and reaches its climactic stage, it is usual for the oil, mining and other basic industries to lead the advance, while utilities and the financial sectors struggle. The drivers here are rising inflation and interest rates – trends that have a tendency to occur at market tops. The financial and utilities sectors have a negative relationship with these variables, while oil, mining and basic industries have a positive relationship.

The key indicator to monitor is how the 'inflationary' sectors are outperforming the 'deflationary' or interest rate-sensitive cyclical sectors as the bull market enters its final stages. When the oil, mining and other basic industry sectors peak out against the underperforming utilities and financial sectors, it is a good sign that the bull market has run its course. At this stage, the smart money that has been riding off the coattails of the inflationary sectors will head for the exit. It pays to follow their lead.

Conclusion: Bull market tops

No one is going to ring a bell to signal a bull market top, but they really don't need to. In the US, sentiment indicators such as excessive fund flows into ETFs and mutual funds, extremely low readings on the contrarian put/call ratio, high readings on the consumer confidence index and low levels of market volatility have proved reliable telltale signs of market tops in the past. Other warning signals worth keeping a close eye on include divergence between price activity and the A/D line and ominous economic signals, such as an inverted yield curve. Also, remember, when Wall Street tops out, the UK stock market is unlikely to be far behind.

" no one is going to ring a bell to signal a bull market top, but they really don't need to, remember, when Wall Street tops out, the UK stock market is unlikely to be far behind "

chapter

2

Bear market bottoms

A ssuming that you have been smart enough to call the top of the
market and left the bull market party without suffering a hang-
over, then you still have to deal with the ensuing bear market.

Bear markets are defined as periods when the stock market falls by 20 per
cent or more. In reality, it is academic whether the fall in share prices is a
correction (a decline of between 10 and 20 per cent) or a fully fledged
bear market. In either case, the losses will be painful if you are on the
wrong side of the trade.

> **buying into an anticipated market recovery too early can be dangerous and financially disastrous**

It is therefore important to know when a bear
market is likely to bottom out as buying into an
anticipated market recovery too early can be dangerous and financially disastrous. Fortunately,
there are ten key trends and signals to look out for
that make life so much easier when trying to identify bear market bottoms.

US bear market bottoms

Trend 1: The history books

Our history books give us some very useful pointers as to when bear markets are likely to end. Let's consider all 24 of the US bear markets in the
past 75 years.

First, bear markets have an uncanny knack of bottoming out in October.
Incredibly, no fewer than 6 of the 24 bear markets have ended in that

❝ bear markets have an uncanny knack of bottoming out in October ... bear markets simply do not end in the fifth year of the decade ❞

month. Second, bear markets simply do not end in the fifth year of the decade. Not a single one has troughed out in a year ending in 5 in the past 100 years.

The odds are good, however, that a bear market will end in the second or eighth year of the decade. These years account for 8 of the 24 bear market bottoms. In other words, almost 60 per cent of the bear markets in the US have bottomed out in either October or the second or eighth year of the decade.

Third, short bear markets (those of less than one year in duration) are like a trip to the dentist. The pain is immediate and it can be severe, but,

❝ short bear markets are like a trip to the dentist. The pain is immediate and it can be severe, but we get over them quickly ❞

we get over them quickly. Since 1932, the average length of a bear market is around 12 months, but, on average, the drop in prices in those 12 months is a stomach-churning 26 per cent. The good news is that almost two thirds of these 24 bear markets have been short, lasting less than one year.

The US presidential cycle is also worth bearing in mind when looking for bear market bottoms (see Chapter 7) as the US stock market has a habit of bottoming out in the first or second years of the presidential term (see Table 2.1).

It may seem a hard task to predict when a bear market bottom will occur, but 75 years of stock market history tell us that the odds are very short that it will either occur in the second or eighth year of the decade, in the month of October or in the first or second years of a presidential term. Armed with that knowledge, timing market bottoms is easier than it may first seem.

Trend 2: Rock bottom valuations

❝ one way to gauge how low valuations will fall is to use the cyclically adjusted price to earnings ratio ❞

One common feature of all the bear market lows in the past eight decades is that valuations are significantly depressed in these troughs. One way to gauge how low valuations will fall is to use the cyclically adjusted price to earnings (PE) ratio, which is the latest market price divided by the average earnings from the market over the

table 2.1 Presidential elections and market troughs

Presidential term	Month and year of market bottom trough	Year during presidential term when market bottomed
1942–1944	April 1942	2nd year
1945–1948	October 1946	2nd year
1949–1952	June 1949	1st year
1953–1956	September 1953	1st year
1957–1960	October 1957	1st year
1961–1964	June 1962	2nd year
1965–1968	October 1966	2nd year
1969–1972	May 1970	2nd year
1973–1976	October 1974	2nd year
1977–1980	March 1978	2nd year
1981–1984	August 1982	2nd year
1985–1988	December 1987	3rd year
1989–1992	October 1990	2nd year
1993–1996	April 1994	2nd year
1997–2000	August 1998	2nd year
2001–2004	October 2002	2nd year
		Average = 22.5 months into presidential term

Source: Marshall D. Nickles, EdD, 'Presidential Elections and Stock Market Cycles,' 2004, Graziadio Business Report, Pepperdine University, http://gbr.pepperdine.edu/043/stocks.html

past 10 years (Murphy, 2008). In the past, bear market bottoms are commonly reached when the adjusted PE ratio falls to around 10. This is also known as the Shiller PE ratio, as it was devised by Yale University professor Robert Shiller (charts and data of the Shiller PE can be viewed at: **www.irrationalexuberance.com**).

To put this into perspective, the cyclically adjusted price to earnings ratio of the S&P 500 was north of 20 as of June 2008, implying that the on-going bear market had yet to hit rock bottom.

Trend 3: Extreme volatility and negative investor sentiment

Just as bull market tops are formed at times of investor complacency, bear market bottoms can occur when there is near panic in the markets. This is the capitulation stage when investors throw in the towel. Moves in the Chicago Board Options Exchange (CBOE) VIX index (see Chapter 1 for details of how the VIX is calculated) into the range 45–50 indicate extreme levels of fear among investors and have been associated with previous major market bottoms. It is therefore worth keep-ing a close eye on the VIX (it can be monitored on the CBOE's website at: **www.cboe.com**).

❝ bear market bottoms can occur when there is near panic in the markets, this is the capitulation stage ❞

Adviser sentiment surveys (such as those con-ducted by financial research company Investors Intelligence – see at: **www.investorsintelligence.com**) are great contrar-ian indicators, too. For instance, the ratio of bullish financial advisers to bearish ones fell below parity in both October 2002 and March 2003 (see Figure 2.1), which indicated that advisers were being too pessimistic about future prospects. These dates also coincided with the bottom of the 2000–2003 bear market.

Similarly, advisers were equally bearish following the extreme sell-off in the US markets in January 2008. This point marked an intermediate low in the bear market, with the S&P 500 Index rallying 14 per cent from those lows to the highs in mid-May 2008.

❝ adviser sentiment surveys ... are great contrarian indicators ... when there have been extreme readings ❞

It is true, though, that advisers can become overly bullish or bearish for great periods of time, during which stock prices can head even lower. Nonetheless, this sentiment index has proved a good contrarian indicator when there have been extreme readings in adviser sentiment.

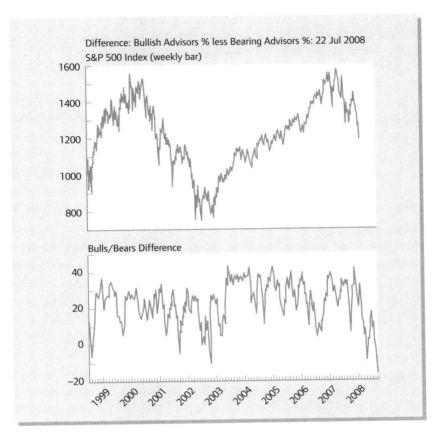

Difference: Bullish Advisors % less Bearing Advisors %: 22 Jul 2008
S&P 500 Index (weekly bar)

Bulls/Bears Difference

figure 2.1 Advisor Sentiment Survey results since 1998

Source: Investors Intelligence

Trend 4: The 200-day moving average test

The 200-day moving average of an index (the average of the closing prices from the past 200 trading days) is one of the most reliable ways of testing whether a market has fallen too far or not. If investors become too risk averse and share prices fall steeply, then the market can fall way below its 200-day moving average.

Research from James Altucher (Thompson, 2008d), a partner at hedge fund Formula Capital, shows that, if you had bought the S&P 500 every time it fell 20 per cent below its 200-day moving average in the past 33 years, then a month later you would have been in profit. This has

> **❝ bear market bottoms are frequently hit when investors have sold the market down to extreme levels, way below its long-term moving average ❞**

happened 34 times since 1975, with every trade a winning one (average gain 10 per cent). The last time this happened was in October 2002, which also signalled the low point of the 2000–2002 bear market.

This is such a great indicator because bear market bottoms are frequently hit when investors have sold the market down to extreme levels, way below its long-term moving average.

Trend 5: Early signs of economic improvement

Teun Draaisma may not be a household name to many, but he is well worth listening to.

The chief equity strategist at US investment bank Morgan Stanley, he came to prominence in June 2007 when he issued a triple sell warning on the stock market a matter of weeks before it topped out. Then, in mid-August – days before the US's central bank, the Federal Reserve, reduced the discount rate, which prompted a surge in US stock prices – he advised investors to start buying equities as his market timing models indicated that the market was heavily oversold and ripe for a rally. Mr Draaisma correctly called the end of that rally at the end of October 2007. He was also successful when he advised that it was time to buy back again in late January 2008.

So, it is well worth taking note of what Mr Draaisma said when he was asked, 'What are the best signs to look out for to confirm improvement in the economy?' Having researched 100 years of US stock market history, Mr Draaisma found that bear markets generally don't hit their final low point until the copper price has bottomed, automotive sales start to rise and inventory levels are low (Murphy, 2008).

> **❝ bear markets generally don't hit their final low point until the copper price has bottomed, automotive sales start to rise and inventory levels are low ❞**

Remember, if the economy is on the way to recovery, so is the stock market. So, here are three key indicators that it is wise to monitor when trying to identify bear market bottoms.

Trend 6: Bond market rally

In past, bear markets' government bonds and corporate bonds have rallied, on average, between 10 and 4 months, respectively, before equity markets finally hit their bottom (Thompson, 2008c). This is sensible as the appetite for corporate debt is likely to rise if investors are confident that the economic recovery (which will feed through to company profits and so reduces default risk in the bond markets) is back on track. Also, as the stock market is a forward-looking discounting mechanism, stock prices will start to rise well before companies start to report that profits are recovering. So, it pays to keep a close eye on movements in the bond markets when trying to identify likely bear market bottoms.

> ❝ government and corporate bonds have rallied ... between 10 and 4 months, respectively, before equity markets finally hit their bottom ❞

Trend 7: McClellan Summation Index

The McClellan Summation Index (MSI) is a popular market breadth indicator that is derived from the number of advancing and declining stocks in an index. It was developed by Sherman and Marian McClellan (**www.mcoscillator.com**).

Over the years, the Index has had an excellent record in identifying major market lows when selling pressure has driven market breadth down to unsustainably low levels (readings on the MSI below minus 500). For instance, the MSI on the Nasdaq Composite Index was at extremely low levels after the US stock markets hit lows in January and March 2008. So, when the MSI started to turn up, it was a signal that market breadth was improving and investors were starting to buy shares in an increasing number of companies. The Index was spot on, with the Nasdaq rallying 23 per cent from mid-March to mid-May 2008. Indeed, in the past eight years, the MSI has only given one false signal when identifying major market lows.

> ❝ the Index has had an excellent record in identifying major market lows ... in the past eight years, the MSI has only given one false signal ❞

Websites such as **www.stockcharts.com** produce daily updates for the Index.

UK bear market bottoms

Since 1825, there have been 21 bear markets in the UK. These have lasted, on average, 35 months, with the UK stock market falling by a third from

" since 1825, there have been 21 bear markets in the UK "

the peak of the previous bull market top to the bottom of the bear market (see Table 2.2). Even though there has been a tendency since the 1950s for UK bear markets to be shorter in length (the majority of the past eight bear markets have ended within nine months), they have been no less severe, with the average peak-to-trough fall still being over 30 per cent.

table 2.2 UK bear markets, 1825–2003

Bear market period	Percentage fall from peak to trough	Duration (months)
March 1825–March 1831	−62.7	72
April 1836–November 1841	−30.3	67
September 1845–October 1848	−37.7	35
November 1865–October 1868	−27.9	35
October 1873–July 1879	−36.1	68
February 1900–March 1909	−20.6	109
April 1911–October 1921	−25.5	126
September 1929–June 1932	−52.3	33
January 1937–July 1940	−39.1	41
July 1957–February 1958	−22.1	7
May 1961–June 1962	−26.7	13
July 1966–November 1966	−18.7	4
February 1969–June 1970	−37.6	16
August 1972–December 1974	−69.7	27
January 1976–October 1976	−28.7	9
May 1979–January 1980	−17.9	8
July 1987–October 1987	−35.9	4
January 1990–October 1990	−19.6	9
July 1998–October 1998	−24.9	2.5
January 2000–March 2003	−50.6	38
June 2007–October 2008*	−43.7	16
Average	**−34.7**	**35**

* Bear market low as of October 2008

Source: *Investors Chronicle*

The greatest problem investors face during bear markets is misplaced optimism. As a series of sucker rallies try to draw them back into the market, it is easy to believe that share prices have bottomed out, only for the next leg of the downturn to unravel. Stock market history is littered with such bear market rallies.

> the greatest problem is misplaced optimism ... it clearly pays to know whether rallies are the real deal or just another false dawn

For instance, in the 3 years after October 1929, the Dow Jones Industrial Average fell about 90 per cent in total, but it enjoyed 5 rallies of between 16 and 48 per cent. More recently, in the 3 years after the dot.com bubble burst in March 2000, the technology-laden Nasdaq fell almost 80 per cent, but still had 4 rallies of at least 22 per cent. Fast forward through the next 8 years and you will see that the Nasdaq plunged by 25 per cent between November 2007 and March 2008 before rallying 23 per cent in the following couple of months (Thompson, 2008a). It clearly pays to know whether these rallies are the real deal or just another false dawn.

Trend 8: UK bear markets retracements

To avoid being drawn into the market too early, our history books reveal some trends that date back over eight decades. The first and most important of these is that there is a correlation between the length and depth of a bear market and the length and depth of the preceding bull market. Namely, the longer the bull market, the deeper the subsequent retracement in share prices.

> since the Great Depression, there have been 21 bull markets in the UK, of which 14 ended within two and a half years ... the bear markets following the seven longer bull markets were far more savage

Stock market historian David Schwartz (2008c; Thompson, 2008a) has discovered that, since the Great Depression, there have been 21 bull markets in the UK, of which 14 ended within two and a half years. In virtually all the subsequent bear markets following these 14 short bull markets, the market fell less than 25 per cent from the peak of the previous bull market to the trough of the bear market.

Mr Schwartz also notes that the bear markets following the seven longer bull markets were far more savage. In 3 of these 7 bear markets, the UK stock market recorded falls of between 25 and 30 per cent, in 2 the market fell by 31–40 per cent, with the other 2 bear markets posting declines of over 40 per cent before bottoming out. This included a hefty 51 per cent fall in the UK stock market between March 2000 and March 2003.

To see how these historical price trends have worked in recent years, let's consider the last bull market in the UK.

When the FTSE All-Share peaked out in June 2007, the bull market had run for a lengthy 51 months, with the Index rising by 119 per cent in this time. During the bear market that followed, the Index subsequently slumped by 43 per cent at its low point in October 2008. So, once again our history books have proved that long-running bull markets are always followed by severe bear markets, with prices dropping by at least 25 per cent as a minimum.

❝ there have been 9 bull markets when the stock market rose by over 100 per cent ... in each of the 9 bear markets that followed the UK share stock market fell by at least 25 per cent ❞

There is another strong price trend Mr Schwartz uncovered that has also stood the test of time. Since the 1930s, there have been 9 bull markets in the UK when the stock market rose by over 100 per cent (Thompson, 2008a), the 2003–2007 bull market being the last occasion that this had happened. It may not be a well-known fact, but, in each of the 9 bear markets that followed these 9 bull markets, the UK stock market fell by at least 25 per cent, including the 2007/2008 bear market.

So the next time the stock market peaks out after a long bull run or when the market has doubled in value, if history is a good guide, we can expect, at the very least, a 25 per cent fall in share prices in the subsequent bear market.

Trend 9: First quarter price falls

❝ there have been 10 occasions when the UK market has fallen by over 7.5 per cent in the first 3 months of the year ... a bear market was running every time ❞

In the past 100 years, there have been 10 occasions when the UK market has fallen by over 7.5 per cent in the first 3 months of the year. Not only was a bear market running in every one of those cases, but nine of those ten bear markets did not bottom out for at least another three months after the end of March. We can thank Mr Schwartz for this gem (Schwartz, 2008a; Thompson, 2008a).

It's relevant to note this now because, in the first quarter of 2008, both the FTSE All-Share and FTSE 100 indices fell by 11 per cent, which is the eleventh occasion the market has fallen by over 7.5 per cent in the first quarter. If history was going to repeat itself, a fully fledged bear market was running and prices had further to fall. In the event, this proved correct, with the UK indices dropping a further 33 per cent by mid-October.

Trend 10: Bull market signal for end of bear market

Understandably, given the hefty price falls seen in bear markets, not everyone will be convinced that the bear market bottom is in place even if the historical price trends above are being followed. More cautious investors may want further confirmation that the bear market has ended.

Fortunately, there is a major buy signal, discovered by Mr Schwartz, that has marked the start of a new bull market on every occasion in the last 14 bull markets. Namely, the UK stock market has risen by at least 8 per cent from its bear market low point in the first 2 months of a new bull market (Schwartz, 2008a; Thompson, 2008a).

❝ as a rule of thumb, bear markets generally end when valuations are low enough to underpin a sustained rally in stock prices ❞

True, it is quite possible that, in the future, a bull market could be under way when prices have risen less than 8 per cent 2 months after a bear market has bottomed out. However, this has yet to happen in any of the 14 bull markets Mr Schwartz analysed.

Conclusion: Bear market bottoms

As a rule of thumb, bear markets generally end when valuations are low enough to underpin a sustained rally in stock prices, sentiment has become overly bearish, bond market investors feel confident enough to start buying corporate bonds again and share prices have retraced a significant proportion of the gains made during the prior bull market. By taking into consideration the ten key indicators outlined in this chapter, spotting bear market bottoms is far less difficult than it may at first appear.

Profiting from a bear market

Some asset classes do fantastically well in bear markets and it has paid to follow these in the past. Research by *Investors Chronicle* (Picarda, 2008) shows that the Swiss franc has been a safe haven for UK investors in previous bear markets. In the past nine bear markets, the currency has risen against sterling by an average of 15.1 per cent with no down years (see Table 2.3). Sterling has also been weak against the euro, falling by 14.7 per cent on average over the course of these bear markets, with it managing to rise in value in only one year. Please note that, pre-2000, the ECU (or European Currency Unit) was used as a proxy for the euro.

> " as safe havens go, gold has had a great track record, in the past nine bear markets, increasing in value by 278 per cent on average "

As safe havens go, gold has had a great track record in the past nine bear markets, increasing in value by 278 per cent on average.

table 2.3   Profiting from a bear market

Year	Percentage change in Swiss franc v. sterling (%)	Percentage change in euro v. sterling (%)	Gold
1969–1970	2.6	27.6	−39.7
1972–1974	13.8	14.8	1367.9
1976	38	54.9	−16.7
1979–1980	2.4	4.5	1058.4
1987	5.9	1.8	6.3
1990	5.7	−24.2	7.1
1998	45.8	32.9	2.2
2000–2003	4.9	2.8	58.3
2007–2008*	17.0	17.0	57.0
Average	**15.1**	**14.7**	**277.9**

* Correct at July 2008

Source: *Investors Chronicle*

Reasons for the phenomenon

The weakness of sterling against the euro and Swiss franc is quite logical as bear markets are associated with periods when the UK economy is generally weak, so investors are more likely to deposit their money in currencies of countries that have economies stronger than the UK's. In turn, there is likely to be less pressure on the interest rates earned on these foreign currency deposits to fall, whereas the Bank of England is likely to try to give the weak UK economy a boost by lowering its interest rates. This certainly seems to be the case during the 2007/2008 UK bear market, with sterling falling by 17 per cent against both the euro and the Swiss franc between June 2007 and April 2008.

❝ interest rate cuts make the yield on dollar deposits less attractive to overseas investors, who are more likely to look elsewhere for better returns ❞

The strong rise in the gold price is also easy to explain. The commodity's strength lies with the US central bank, the Federal Reserve, making significant cuts to interest rates, as it did during the 2000–2003 bear market and again during the 2007–2008 bear market. These interest rate cuts make the yield on dollar deposits less attractive to overseas investors, who are more likely to look elsewhere for better returns.

❝ the Swiss franc is a natural safe haven and it would be the preferred home for sterling deposits in a UK equity bear market ❞

In turn, this puts pressure on the currency. As the gold price is denominated in dollars, investors buy the commodity both as a hedge against a worsening outlook for inflation (which could be stoked by the cuts in US interest rates) and as a natural hedge against further weakness in the dollar. That is exactly what happened between June 2007 and March 2008 when the London spot gold price increased from $656 an ounce to $1032 – a rise of 57 per cent.

trading strategy 1

Buy Swiss francs and gold

The Swiss franc is a natural safe haven and it would be the preferred home for sterling deposits in a UK equity bear market. Gold has its attractions too, especially in the face of dollar weakness. So, a diversified strategy of buying Swiss francs and gold bullion at the start of a UK bear market is recommended.

▶

One way to buy gold is via Exchange Traded Funds (ETFs) that track the price of the commodity. ETFs listed on the London Exchange include ETF Securities Gold (TIDM: BULL). The product is exempt from Stamp Duty on purchase and is traded in the same way as any other share listed on the London market.

Daylight robbery

magine being able to predict on a Friday afternoon how stock markets are going to perform on a Monday morning. It would be a licence to print money. In fact, it's a licence that the seriously smart money have been keeping to themselves – until now.

> " it may seem far-fetched, but it is possible to make money from stock markets around the time when the clocks go forward or back "

It may seem far-fetched, but it is possible to make money from the stock markets around the time when the clocks go forward or back (called daylight saving in the USA). The reason for this is simple – our reactions to changes in our own body clocks, or, as the medical profession like to put it, the fact that we desynchronise.

The joys of spring?

As anyone who has suffered a bad night's sleep knows all too well, our behaviour the next day can be dogged by weariness, lethargy and, in some cases, despondency. True, the lack of one hour's sleep when the clocks go forward one hour in the spring and the gain of an extra hour's rest when they go back one hour in the autumn is hardly a major sleep imbalance. However, academics have shown that even minor sleep imbalances can cause errors in judgement, anxiety, impatience and loss of attention. Insurance companies and car drivers know this to their cost: research confirms that

> " academics have shown that even minor sleep imbalances can cause errors in judgement ... it is logical that they could affect us when making financial decisions "

there is a significant increase in car accidents following both clocks going forward in the spring and when they go back in the autumn. Long-haul air travellers are victims of this phenomenon, too: sufferers of jet lag show reduced problem solving ability and response times.

So, if changes in our sleep patterns can affect us in our every day lives, then it is logical that they could affect our behaviour when it comes to making financial decisions. That is exactly what academics have found.

❝stock market returns on the first business day of the week following the clocks changing in the spring produced larger falls … compared to other weekends❞

Academics Mark Kamstra, Lisa Kramer and Maurice Levi (2000) found that stock market returns on the first business day of the week following the clocks changing in the spring produced larger falls in the market compared to other weekends in the year.

In fact, taking data over a 30-year period, from 1967 to 1998, the academics found that the mean negative return on the first trading day following the clocks going forward in the spring was between two and five times greater than that following an ordinary weekend. It is not just a local phenomenon either – the sample included the Nasdaq Composite, S&P 500 and New York Stock Exchange Composite indices in the US, Tokyo Stock Exchange 300 in Japan, Dax 30 in Germany and FTSE All-Share Index in the UK.

The problem with apparent stock market anomalies is that, as soon as market players become aware of their existence, they take advantage of it and so the anomaly quickly disappears. To test whether or not the clocks

❝to test whether or not the clocks changing has affected the UK stock market in recent years, I tested the theory … the results are staggering❞

changing has affected the UK stock market in recent years, I tested the theory on the past 27 years, for the period between 1981 and 2008. The results are staggering.

First, there is a definite trend for the UK market to fall on the first trading day after the clocks go forward one hour on the last Sunday in March (see Table 3.1). In fact, since 1981, the FTSE All-Share Index – which consists of the FTSE 100, FTSE 250 and FTSE Small Cap indices – has fallen no fewer

than 17 times in these past 27 years, producing an average negative return of 0.78 per cent on those down days. By contrast, there were only 10 of those days that turned out to be up days – producing an average return of 0.89 per cent. In aggregate, investors who had been holding an

table 3.1 Performance of FTSE All-Share Index post clocks going forward (1981–2007)

Year	Percentage change in FTSE All-Share on day after clocks change in March
1981	−0.30
1982	−0.79
1983	−0.14
1984	−1.10
1985	0.06
1986	0.95
1987	−2.04
1988	−1.21
1989	0.59
1990	0.46
1991	1.00
1992	−0.45
1993	−0.23
1994	0.05
1995	−0.06
1996	0.37
1997	−1.54
1998	−0.38
1999	1.53
2000	−0.53
2001	2.83
2002	−0.27
2003	−2.39
2004	1.02
2005	−0.12
2006	−0.99
2007	−0.67
Average return	**−0.16**
Up	10
Down	17
Average up gain (%)	0.89
Average down loss (%)	−0.78

Source: Thomson Reuters Datastream

index tracking fund would have shown an average loss of 0.16 per cent on the last Monday of March. By the same token, short selling the UK stock market prior to its close on the preceding Friday would have produced an average gain of 0.16 per cent at close of trading on the following Monday.

❝ the trend for the UK stock market to fall on the first Monday following the clocks going forward in spring has accelerated in recent years ❞

What's more, the trend for the UK stock market to fall on the first Monday following the clocks going forward in spring has accelerated in recent years. In fact, since 1997, there have only been 3 up days, albeit strong up days, but the market has fallen on 8 occasions – producing an average loss of 0.86 per cent – in the past 11 years.

Reasons for the phenomenon

It's worth bearing in mind that the last Monday in March will always be during the final week of the first quarter. That means there is the potential for any adverse stock movements to be the result of fund managers window dressing their portfolios ahead of the end of the quarter. Asset managers could be tempted to bank gains on profitable holdings, leading to short-term selling pressure, as well as dumping some of their poorest-performing holdings as well. That means they avoid the ignominy of having to report these 'dog' holdings to the shareholders in these funds.

❝ there is the potential for any adverse stock movements to be the result of fund managers window dressing their portfolios ahead of the end of the quarter ❞

In addition, private investors get in on the act, too, as the last week of March is very close to the end of the tax year. So, there is the possibility that investors could be inclined to bank profits to crystalise gains for capital gains tax reasons at this time.

There is another rational explanation for the market being more inclined to fall on the last Monday in March: changes to the constituents of the FTSE 100 and FTSE 250 indices following the quarterly FTSE International Committee's Quarterly Index Review. The Committee meets on the first Wednesday of March, June, September and December to decide which companies will be promoted and relegated from these two blue-chip indices (these indices account for over 90 per cent of the value of the FTSE All-Share Index). Changes to the constituents of these indices come into effect 12 days later. As a result, fund managers tracking

> **fund managers tracking the FTSE 100 and 250 ... have no choice but to sell holdings in companies being relegated from the indices and buy those entering them**

the FTSE 100 and 250 indices will have no choice but to sell holdings in companies being relegated from the indices and to buy those entering them.

So, although the selling pressure from tracker fund managers will have ended by the time the clocks go forward on the last Sunday in March, it is quite possible that there is a short-term momentum price effect, whereby companies being relegated suffer further selling from other shareholders. By contrast, companies being promoted will have already seen upward movements in their share prices – hence their being promoted, as the changes are based on the market capitalisations of the companies on the date the FTSE International Review Committee meets. For example, asset managers benchmarked against these indices will have been buying shares in advance of the index changes to rebalance their portfolios, while momentum investors will have cottoned on to the possibility of these companies being promoted and so will have bought ahead of the Quarterly Index Review.

The net effect is that, in the short-term, the momentum from selling pressure, following a company's relegation from the indices, has greater potential to depress share prices than the upward buying momentum on company's being promoted has to raise prices further. As the FTSE International Quarterly Review of constituents of the FTSE 100 and FTSE 250 takes place in the second half of March, then it is reasonable to expect some fall-out from the changes to impact the indices at the end of March.

> **it is reasonable to expect some fall-out from the changes to impact the indices at the end of March**

Needless to say, whatever the case, the result is the same – the odds are heavily skewed in favour of the market falling on the last Monday in March.

Autumn sun shines on investors

Investors may have the spring blues at the end of March, but the opposite is true when the clocks go forward one hour on the last Sunday in October.

The market has risen no fewer than 19 times in the past 27 years on the Monday after the clocks have changed on the last Sunday in October (see Table 3.2). The average gain is 0.77 per cent on these 19 up days compared with a loss of 1.55 per cent on the 8 down days. On average, there was a

table 3.2   Performance of FTSE All-Share Index post clocks going back
(1981–2007)

Year	Percentage change in FTSE All-Share Index on day after clocks change in October
1981	0.23
1982	2.15
1983	1.46
1984	0.39
1985	0.22
1986	0.49
1987	−7.16
1988	−0.18
1989	1.30
1990	−0.03
1991	1.43
1992	−0.19
1993	−0.28
1994	0.42
1995	0.35
1996	0.10
1997	−2.26
1998	0.28
1999	0.43
2000	0.33
2001	−1.82
2002	0.96
2003	0.29
2004	0.98
2005	2.07
2006	−0.52
2007	0.62
Average return	**0.08**
Up	19
Down	8
Average up gain (%)	0.77
Average down loss (%)	−1.55

Source: Thomson Reuters Datastream

❝ even in the face of extreme market falls the market has still managed, on average, to rise on the last Monday in October ❞ modest gain of 0.08 per cent on the last Monday in October over this 27-year period. However, this only tells part of the story as those eight down days included extremely rare periods of stock market turbulence, such as the 1987 stock market crash, the Asian Market crisis in 1997 and a volatile period of trading during the last equity bear market in 2001. In other words, even in the face of very extreme market falls during these three years, the market has still managed, on average, to rise on the last Monday in October.

Interestingly, the trend for the market to rise on the last Monday in October has been more marked in recent years. Since 1994, there have been only 3 down days in this period compared to 11 up days – the latter producing an average daily gain of 0.62 per cent.

Reasons for the phenomenon

❝ just as desynchronised sleep may cause investors to be more cautious and risk averse in the spring, the extra hour's sleep in the autumn can have the opposite effect ❞ Perhaps the extra hour in bed makes us feel more energetic and places us in a more positive frame of mind. This explanation for the market's tendency to rise on the day after the clocks go back one hour in the autumn, though clearly subjective, certainly has some credence if you consider that financial market participants – such as asset managers, stockbrokers, analysts and stock traders – work longer hours during the normal working week than the national average, so are far more likely to spend less time sleeping. For example, equity traders in London will be at their desks well before 7 a.m. in the morning, ahead of briefings by their brokerage sales team and the start of pre-market trading.

So, just as desynchronised sleep may cause investors and traders alike to be more cautious and risk averse in the spring – the lack of sleep having a negative effect on their mental state – it is rational to believe that the extra hour's sleep in the autumn can have the opposite effect.

❝ the UK market has had more up days than down days during the last five trading days of October ❞ In addition, it is worth noting that October has been one of the best performing months in the past 15 years in the UK market, with the FTSE 100 index posting no fewer than 13 up years and an average monthly return of 0.3 per cent at this time. No other month has recorded as many up years as this.

There is a positive seasonal bias, too, as the period from the start of May to the end of October has traditionally produced poor returns for investors. Indeed, since 1990 the FTSE All-Share Index has produced an average return of just 0.25 per cent in this 6-month period. By comparison, in the past 17 years, the UK market has posted an average gain of 7.1 per cent between the start of November and the end of April.

Therefore, investors who are aware of the fact that the winter and spring months traditionally perform the best will be more inclined to start buying equities at the end of October. This partly explains why the month has had more up years than any other in the past 15 years, but also why the market is more likely to rise than fall on the final Monday at the end of the month after the clocks go back one hour. Moreover, the figures support this in no uncertain terms. Since 1984, the UK market has had more up days than down days during the last five trading days of October.

> there is a definite trend for the market to rise on the day after the clocks go back in the autumn and fall on the day after they go forward in the spring

trading strategy 2

Make the most of spring

Irrespective of whether you believe that desynchronised sleep can affect financial markets, what is not in doubt is that there is a definite trend for the market to rise on the day after the clocks go back in the autumn and fall on the day after they go forward in the spring.

True, some or all of the other factors outlined above may, and probably do, play their part in skewing investment returns in this way, but what is clear is that this trend has been strengthening in recent years. That is not only reassuring but it also offers investors the opportunity to profit by opening a short position on the UK market before it closes on the last Friday in March, relatively safe in the knowledge that the odds are heavily skewed in favour of the market falling on the following Monday.

One way to execute this trade is through a down spread bet on the FTSE 100 through a spread betting firm. In the UK, these include companies such as City Index, IG Index, Capital Spreads, CMC Markets and Cantor Index. Profits from spread betting are currently tax free in the UK and you can place a bet from as little as a £1 per point on movements in the index. Please note that the FTSE 100 has a weighting of over 75 per cent in the FTSE All-Share Index so most investors prefer to trade the FTSE 100 as there are far more options for buying or selling the index short.

Interestingly, even in 2008 – when the FTSE 100 actually rose modestly from 5692 at the close on Friday 28 March to 5702 at the close on Monday 31 March – the short trade would still have worked. That's because, in the first two hours of that Monday morning, the Index dropped over 100 points before recovering all the losses later in the day. Nimble traders opening shorts on the Index just before the close on Friday 28 March had the opportunity to bank a near 2 per cent gain after the market opened on Monday.

trading strategy 3

Have an Indian summer

The trading strategy in the autumn is to open a long position on the UK market shortly before the FTSE 100 closes on the last Friday in October and aim to bank profits the following Monday. With 11 up days and only 3 down days in the past 14 years, the odds – as well as seasonal factors – are heavily weighted towards the market rising the day after the clocks go back an hour.

In this case, you are buying the FTSE 100 so are placing an up spread bet on every point movement in the Index. Alternatively, you can buy an exchange traded fund (ETF) that tracks the performance of the FTSE 100 with each 1 per cent movement in the Index, translating to a 1 per cent movement in the value of the ETF. ETFs listed on the London Stock Exchange include those issued by Lyxor (TIDM: L100), a subsidiary of French investment bank Société Générale, Deutsche Bank (TIDM: XUKX) and Barclays iShares (TIDM: ISF). ETFs can be bought or sold through stockbrokers in the same way as shares in any listed company.

❝ with 11 up days and only 3 down days in the past 14 years, the odds ... are heavily weighted towards the market rising the day after the clocks go back an hour ❞

4

Built on solid foundations

The nineteenth-century American author Mark Twain is attributed with saying, 'History doesn't repeat itself, but it does rhyme.' However, if Mr Twain or whoever it was had been privy to one of the stock market's most profitable trading secrets, he may have been persuaded to change his mind. That's because there is an amazing phenomenon – the first quarter housebuilder effect – that has repeated itself year after year for the best part of three decades, generating huge trading profits for those in the know.

> **❝ if Mr Twain had been privy to one of the stock market's most profitable trading secrets, he may have been persuaded to change his mind ❞**

First quarter housebuilder effect

Here's how it works. At the start of the year, all you have to do is buy a selection of the UK's largest housebuilders and hold them for three months. At the end of March, phone up your stockbroker or spread betting company and close your positions, but, most importantly, tell them to send you a cheque with your profits. It may sound simple, but if you had followed this trading strategy for the past 29 years, you would have made a profit in the first quarter of the year on no fewer than 24 occasions – a strike rate of over 82 per cent. Moreover, the average quarterly gain has been a very impressive 10.7 per cent each year, even allowing for the 5 down years in this period.

> **❝ at the end of March, phone up your stockbroker or spread betting company and close your positions, but tell them to send you a cheque with your profits ❞**

Superior investment return

To illustrate this stock market phenomenon, let's compare the first quarter returns on the UK housebuilding sector and the FTSE All-Share Index (see Table 4.1). It can be seen that the housebuilders not only outperform the benchmark UK index, on average, more years than not (24 up years since 1980 compared to 21 up years for the FTSE All-Share Index) but also the quarterly return on the sector is significantly higher at 10.7 per cent compared to the average first quarter return of 3.8 per cent on the UK market (see column three in Table 4.1). That is reason enough to follow this trading strategy.

Pair trading

That is very good, but it gets better. That's because we can also pair trade the housebuilding sector against the UK market by buying shares in the housebuilders and simultaneously short selling the market over the first quarter (see the case study on page 43). Short selling the market is when you place a down spread bet on the Index, so this short trade makes a profit when the Index falls in value, but a loss if it rises.

The easiest way to do this is through a spread betting firm. In the UK, these include IG Index, City Index, Capital Spreads CMC Markets and Cantor Index. All these companies make markets in the FTSE 100, which accounts for around 75 per cent of the weighting in the FTSE All-Share Index, so tracks the Index very closely. Most investors prefer to trade the FTSE 100 Index rather than the FTSE All-Share Index. A down bet is simple to execute and you can place a bet for as little as £1 per point movement on the FTSE 100.

if you had bought a selection of shares in the housebuilders at the start of January each year and simultaneously sold short the FTSE 100, the average return has been an eye-watering 6.9 per cent

Since 1980, if you had bought a selection of shares in the housebuilders at the start of January each year and simultaneously sold short through a down spread bet the same value of the FTSE 100, this trade would have produced a positive return during the first quarter in no fewer than 25 of the past 29 years. The average return from this trading strategy has been an eye-watering 6.9 per cent (see column four in Table 4.1). Remember, this trading strategy of buying the housebuilders and selling the FTSE 100 Index to the same value not only improves the chances of generating a positive return during the first quarter but it also, importantly, reduces investment risk, too.

table 4.1 FTSE 350 housebuilding index's first quarter performance since 1980

Year	Percentage change in housebuilding index (%)	Percentage change in FTSE All-Share Index (%)	Pair trade (%)
1980	6.6	4.6	2.0
1981	53.5	6.0	47.5
1982	18.0	4.3	13.7
1983	15.9	7.8	8.1
1984	4.9	11.4	−6.5
1985	−10.7	3.9	−14.6
1986	30.1	18.7	11.4
1987	25.6	20.2	5.4
1988	10.9	3.0	7.9
1989	16.8	16.1	0.7
1990	−7.0	−7.4	0.4
1991	18.6	15.6	3.0
1992	7.5	−1.4	8.9
1993	13.3	3.2	10.1
1994	−4.0	−7.1	3.1
1995	2.7	1.1	1.6
1996	5.1	2.2	2.9
1997	5.9	4.3	1.6
1998	21.5	15.4	6.1
1999	34.5	8.3	26.2
2000	−16.2	−4.1	−12.1
2001	14.8	−9.1	23.9
2002	12.0	1.3	10.7
2003	0.4	−8.3	8.7
2004	19.0	−0.5	19.5
2005	8.1	1.7	6.4
2006	8.3	7.1	1.2
2007	0.1	1.9	−1.8
2008	−6.5	−10.9	4.4
Quarterly return	**10.7**	**3.8**	**6.9**
Up years	24	21	25
Down years	5	8	4

Source: Thomson Reuters Datastream

Please note that, following a series of takeovers in the housebuilding sector, there are now only seven UK listed housebuilders in the FTSE 350 Index. Ranked by market value, these are Berkeley Group (£900 million market value), Persimmon, Bellway, Bovis Homes, Barratt Developments, Redrow and Taylor Wimpey (£150 million market value).

The data in Table 4.1 uses the Thomson Datastream housebuilder price index (HOMESUK) to track the performance of this subsector of the stock market. However, as the seven companies are now classified as part of the diversified FTSE Household Goods sector, it is not possible to buy an ETF that tracks the housebuilding sector. The best way to gain exposure to the housebuilding sector is to simply buy ordinary shares in the companies.

---

case study

Pair trading in practice

Let's say that you bought £5500-worth of shares in a selection of the housebuilders on 2 January and those shareholdings rose by 10.7 per cent in value by the end of March. That has been the average return for the sector in the first quarter over the past three decades. So, your holding would be showing a profit of £588 and would be worth £6088 at the end of March.

On 2 January you would also short sell the UK stock market through a down bet on the FTSE 100. Let's say that the Index was trading at 5500 on 2 January. A down spread bet of £1 a point would mean that, for every 1 per cent movement in the Index, you would make or lose £55. Similarly, for every 1 per cent movement in the housebuilders, you would make or lose £55. Therefore, you would have the same amount of capital at risk in each of these two trades. That's important because this long–short investment strategy is based on the fact that the housebuilders are likely to outperform the FTSE 100 in the first quarter. The term 'long–short' simply means that you are a buyer in one of the two trades – so are holding a 'long' position – and, simultaneously, a seller in the other trade – holding a 'short' position.

If the FTSE 100 rises by 3.8 per cent between 2 January and 31 March – the average return of the UK stock market in this three-month period over the past three decades – then the Index would be trading at 5709 at the end of March. So, your down spread bet would be showing a loss of £209 at the end of March because the Index has risen by 209 points and you have bet £1 a point that it would *fall* in value. However, the profit of £588 on the holding of shares in the housebuilders more than compensates for the £209 loss on the down bet, giving you a net profit of £379 at the end of March.

Reducing investment risk

Granted, the 6.9 per cent net quarterly return from the investment strategy outlined above is less than the 10.7 per cent return that you would have made by simply buying a selection of the UK's housebuilders at the start of January (see Table 4.1, column 2), but a quick glance at the results in 2008 illustrates why this long–short trading strategy has its merits.

To recap, the UK stock market fell off a cliff in the first three months of 2008 as sub-prime mortgage losses at investment banks, concerns over a US recession and a European economic slowdown spooked investors. In fact, both the FTSE 100 and FTSE All-Share indices ended the first quarter down almost 11 per cent – the UK stock market's worst return by far in this 3-month period for the past 3 decades. The housebuilding sector fell into negative territory, too – falling by 6.5 per cent in the first 3 months of 2008.

> even in the face of this savage sell-off across all global equity markets, a pair trade of buying the housebuilders and short selling the FTSE 100 still produced a positive net return of 4.4 per cent

However, even in the face of this savage sell-off across all global equity markets, the pair trade of buying the housebuilders and short selling the FTSE 100 still produced a positive net return of 4.4 per cent. Very few asset managers ended the first quarter of 2008 in profit, so the 4.4 per cent gain on this pair trade was one that nearly all investors would have taken.

Risk aversion

The 2008 experience also highlights the risk averse nature of this long–short trade. Namely, if markets are rising – as they traditionally do during the seasonally strong winter months – then, given the even stronger seasonal bias of the housebuilding sector, the odds are heavily skewed towards the sector outperforming the market as a whole. However, if markets are falling in the first quarter – as they have done during 8 of the past 29 years – then the housebuilding sector is far less likely to fall with the market. In fact, there have been 4 years – 1992, 2001, 2003 and 2004 – when the UK stock market fell in the first 3 months of the year, but the housebuilding sector still managed to produce a positive return. In these instances, investors would have made gains on both sides of the pair trade, with the holding of housebuilding shares rising in value and the down spread bet on the FTSE 100 also making a profit.

> if markets are rising the odds are heavily skewed towards the sector outperforming the market as a whole

Reasons for the phenomenon

It is not difficult to find rational reasons for the existence of this stock market phenomenon. First, housebuilding is a seasonal business and news flow and annual sales are firmly skewed towards the all important spring selling season. Because there is greater media coverage at this time of year, there is increased investor interest in housebuilders as investors focus on price trends and the strength of the underlying housing market. In addition, the UK listed housebuilding sector, which has been consolidating in recent years, has a firm bias towards reporting financial results in the first quarter. That is because the majority of the companies have calendar or January year ends, so they release preliminary results and outlook statements in March. This, in turn, focuses investor attention on the merits of the sector.

> **❛❛ there is another reason for the sector outperforming the general market in the first quarter: this is when 'cyclical' or 'value' stocks do well ❜❜**

There is another reason for the sector outperforming the general market in the first quarter: this time of the year is when 'cyclical' or 'value' stocks do well. The term 'value' refers to shares that offer above average dividend yields and are generally not highly rated when the market value of a company is compared to its after tax profits and net assets. Moreover, these shares are in sectors that are traditionally 'cyclical' so are very sensitive to changes in macroeconomic conditions.

Housebuilders have for years been trading on below market average earnings multiples, while offering above market dividend yields. Aside from the period 2005–2007 (which, in hindsight, marked the all-time peak of the sector on the back of heightened mergers and acquisition activity), it was customary for the share prices of the UK's major players to trade in line with their net asset values. As a result, the sector falls firmly into the 'value investing' category, which does very well in the winter months.

Fourth quarter housebuilding effect

> **❛❛ when investors become aware of a stock market phenomenon, there is a tendency for them to jump the gun and buy in early ❜❜**

Generally, when investors become aware of a stock market phenomenon, there is a tendency for them to jump the gun and buy in early to try and profit from the expected future buying activity. To a certain extent, in recent years, this has been happening with the housebuilder first quarter effect as some investors have been buying into the sector in the fourth quarter, safe in the knowledge that other investors intend buying in the first quarter. This can be seen in Table 4.2, which highlights performance of the housebuilding

❝ part of the first quarter effect in both 2006 and 2007 had been hijacked by investors who bought shares early in the final quarter of the previous year ❞

sector and the FTSE All-Share Index in the fourth quarter and the return from a long–short pair trade.

In both 2005 and 2006, the housebuilders produced thumping gains in the fourth quarter – 28 per cent and 17.3 per cent, respectively – buoyed by gains during the month of December, in particular. This was way above the average fourth quarter sector return of 5.1 per cent in the past 3 decades. Interestingly, the first quarter performance from the sector that followed in 2006 and 2007 – gains of 8.3 per cent and 0.1 per cent, respectively – were way below the 10.7 per cent first quarter return we have seen, on average, since 1980. In other words, part of the first quarter effect in both 2006 and 2007 had been hijacked by investors who decided to jump the gun and bought housebuilder shares in the final quarter of the previous year.

In a similar way, there were also strong gains in the housebuilding sector in the fourth quarters of 2000 and 2001: returns above 20 per cent were

❝ remember, it has produced a profit in 25 of the past 29 years, with the average quarterly gain being 6.9 per cent ❞

posted in both final quarters. However, in 2001 and 2002, respectively, the sector still managed to post a healthy double digit first quarter return. The logical conclusion is that, as more investors have become aware of this first quarter trading strategy, then there has been a tendency for them to jump the gun by buying in the final quarter.

trading strategy 4

First quarter trading

Even though some smart investors appear to have distorted the price behavior of the housebuilding sector in the first quarter by buying early in the final quarter of the year, this has not affected the favoured first quarter pair trade of simultaneously buying a selection of the housebuilders and short selling the FTSE 100 to the same value. This is still a very profitable strategy and, for the risk averse investor, is the preferred first quarter trade. Remember, it has produced a profit in 25 of the past 29 years, with the average quarterly gain being 6.9 per cent. It even made a profit during the bear market of 2008!

table 4.2 FTSE 350 housebuilding index's fourth quarter performance since 1980

Year	Percentage change in housebuilding index (%)	Percentage change in FTSE All-Share Index (%)	Pair trade (%)
1980	−2.9	0.7	−3.6
1981	0.4	12.4	−12.0
1982	17.2	5.6	11.6
1983	1.4	5.6	−4.2
1984	13.0	10.7	2.3
1985	13.0	9.1	3.9
1986	4.9	8.7	−3.8
1987	−20.4	−28.0	7.6
1988	−7.4	−2.1	−5.3
1989	0.3	3.0	−2.7
1990	19.5	7.3	12.2
1991	−22.2	−6.2	−16.0
1992	25.3	13.1	12.2
1993	14.8	11.6	3.2
1994	−5.2	0.7	−5.9
1995	18.5	4.0	14.5
1996	0.6	3.5	−3.0
1997	−11.0	−1.8	−9.2
1998	6.6	14.0	−7.4
1999	9.2	14.7	−5.5
2000	20.4	−1.5	21.9
2001	20.6	7.8	12.8
2002	−7.8	5.1	−12.9
2003	4.0	8.9	−4.9
2004	5.5	6.1	−0.6
2005	28.0	3.7	24.3
2006	17.3	5.6	11.7
2007	−21.8	−0.9	−20.9
Quarterly return	5.1	4.3	0.8
Up years	20	22	12
Down years	8	6	16

Source: Thomson Reuters Datastream

Fourth quarter trading

It is worth noting that we can also jump the gun and buy into the housebuilding sector in the fourth quarter – December, in particular. The plan here is to play a waiting game. That is because the sector has fallen no fewer than eight times in the final quarter of the year since 1980, so a strategy of simply buying shares in the housebuilders at the end of September is far riskier than our first quarter pair trade.

Moreover, with an average fourth quarterly return of 5.1 per cent since 1980, the return on the housebuilders in the fourth quarter is less than half of what the sector has produced in the first quarter. The modest outperformance of the sector in the final quarter of the year (5.1 per cent sector return compared to a 4.3 per cent on the FTSE All-Share Index since 1980) hardly makes up for the increased risk of holding the shares in a down year.

Taking all these factors into consideration, the optimum fourth quarter trading strategy is to wait until the end of November and buy into the housebuilding sector in the first sustained rally. If there is no rally, then simply don't buy – just wait until the start of January to play trading strategy 4. If there is a sector rally in late November or December, however, this trade has its merits as we know that December is the best-performing month of the year, so the chances of both the stock market *and* the housebuilding sector rising are weighted in our favour.

At the end of the year, the shareholding in the housebuilders should be showing a profit, so the second part of this trade happens at the end of December. Then, short sell the FTSE 100 – through a down spread bet to the same value as the shareholding of housebuilders – to take advantage of the anticipated outperformance of the sector against the market in the first quarter. At the end of March, sell the shareholding of housebuilders and close out the spread bet on the FTSE 100.

❝ the optimum fourth quarter trading strategy is to wait until the end of November and buy into the housebuilding sector in the first sustained rally ❞

5

Seasonal investing and seasonal affective disorder

The nineteenth-century poet John Keats wrote: 'Four seasons fill the measure of the year; there are four seasons in the mind of man' ('The Human Seasons', 1819). The same is true when it comes to playing the stock market successfully. Investors not only have to know when is the best time to be invested in the market, but also when to take a break on the sidelines. Like the seasons, the performance of sectors also changes throughout the year.

Seasonal investing

The City saying 'Sell in May and go away', to come back to the markets after St Leger Day (the last major horse race of the flat season) in September, certainly has merit. The six-month period from the start of May to the end of October is by far the worst time of the year to be invested in the market. In this six-month period, the FTSE All-Share Index has risen, on average, by a pitiful 0.25 per cent since 1990.

❝ the stock market regularly performs poorly in the second and third quarters of the year before jumping back into life in the final quarter and the first three months of the following year ❞

By contrast the six-month period from the start of November to the end of April has recorded an average gain of 7.1 per cent in the past 17 years. Consequently, the stock market regularly performs poorly in the second and third quarters of the year before jumping back into life in the final quarter and the first three months of the following year (see Table 5.1). There are sound reasons for this.

table 5.1 Quarterly performance of FTSE All-Share Index since 1980

Year	First quarter	Second quarter	Third quarter	Fourth quarter
1980	4.61	12.13	7.69	0.68
1981	5.99	3.50	−13.13	12.43
1982	4.30	−1.16	12.09	5.64
1983	7.78	11.40	−2.92	5.60
1984	11.41	−6.96	9.87	10.65
1985	3.92	−3.35	5.15	9.05
1986	18.68	0.64	−5.75	8.67
1987	20.19	14.83	4.84	−28.01
1988	3.05	7.39	−1.74	−2.08
1989	16.14	2.37	6.16	3.01
1990	−7.45	5.05	−17.85	7.28
1991	15.60	−2.69	9.02	−6.18
1992	−1.35	3.83	−0.84	13.07
1993	3.25	1.72	5.18	11.66
1994	−7.15	−6.31	3.25	0.69
1995	1.13	5.52	6.79	4.00
1996	2.24	0.70	4.78	3.53
1997	4.27	4.04	12.38	−1.79
1998	15.37	−1.37	−14.53	14.00
1999	8.26	1.77	−4.08	14.70
2000	−4.06	−2.60	0.00	−1.50
2001	−9.13	0.62	−14.21	7.84
2002	1.33	−11.51	−20.40	5.12
2003	−8.34	13.57	2.86	8.86
2004	−0.47	1.44	1.93	6.12
2005	1.96	4.17	7.25	3.69
2006	7.06	−2.64	2.79	5.61
2007	1.90	3.68	−2.56	−0.91
Quarterly return	4.3	2.1	0.1	4.3
Up years	21	19	17	22
Down years	7	9	11	6

Source: Thomson Reuters Datastream

Economic recession

Economic data suggests that the winter is a risky time of the year to be invested in the market, with real GDP falling by an average of 4.9 per cent in the first quarter in the past 40 years, having risen strongly in the final three months of the previous year – a fact obscured by the seasonal adjustment of economic statistics.

> **if winter creates economic risks, we should expect the return from holding shares to be higher in winter months to offset the greater risks being taken on**

Some economists believe that these seasonal variations can have long-lasting effects, accounting for half of all business cycle fluctuations. So, if winter creates economic risks, we should expect the return from holding shares to be higher in winter months to offset the greater risks being taken on.

Seasonal affective disorder

A variant of seasonal affective disorder (SAD) probably plays its part, too. As the nights get longer in September and October, investors may become more risk averse as their anxiety increases. Remember that September is one of the worst-performing months of the year on both sides of the Atlantic (see Chapter 19). In the UK, the stock market has fallen in September by an average of 1.3 per cent in the past 4 decades. Consequently, shares become cheap by the end of October, which entices buyers back in and so helps boost returns in the seasonally strong November to April period.

> **shares become cheap by the end of October, which entices buyers back in and so helps boost returns in the seasonally strong November to April period**

This kind of SAD also has the reverse effect in the spring, giving the stock market a lift when days become longer and lighter during March and April – two of the strongest months of the year. However, the bumper returns enjoyed during winter and spring mean that the stock market may struggle to make decent headway during the summer and autumn months.

Academic research is supportive of the existence of a SAD effect. In a paper for the Federal Reserve Bank of Atlanta, academics Mark Kamstra, Lisa Kramer and Maurice Levi (2003) found:

The existence of an important effect of seasonal affective disorder on stock market returns around the world in every northern country we consider. Evidence suggests that the impact of SAD in the southern hemisphere is out of phase by six months, relative to the north.

The winter blues theory has merit if we consider that in Australia, where the seasons are six months out of step with those in the UK, the stock market performs less strongly during the UK's winter and spring months, but outperforms it during the UK's summer and autumn. In the past 35 years, the UK market has outperformed the Australian market, on average, by 4.2 per cent between 31 October and 30 April, but has under-performed the Australian market by 3.7 per cent between 30 April and 31 October (see Table 5.2).

> ❝ in Australia, where the seasons are six months out of step with those in the UK, the stock market performs less strongly during the UK's winter and spring months, but outperforms it during the UK's summer and autumn ❞

Earnings revisions

Even if you don't buy the SAD effect, then there is another factor that certainly has a cyclical impact on share prices: analyst earnings revisions. It is in the nature of analysts to be optimistic and so their forecasts are biased towards companies growing earnings over time. When investors look at companies' earnings estimates at the end of the calendar year, they will inevitably assume growth in the next year's profits. As a result of this optimistic outlook going forward, company valuations appear cheaper than they did six months previously, which helps to drive share prices higher into the new year.

> ❝ if analysts have been overly bullish with their estimates, then this is the first opportunity they have to rein in these forecasts ... investors react by becoming more cautious ❞

The problem is that not all companies will hit these optimistic earnings estimates. A high per-centage of UK listed companies release financial results between mid-February and the end of May, so if analysts have been overly bullish with their estimates, then this is the first opportunity they have to rein in these forecasts. In turn, investors react by becoming more cautious and turn to more defensive and less cyclical sectors over the summer months.

table 5.2 Differences in seasonal returns from FTSE All-Share Index and Australian All Ordinaries Index

Year	Difference in winter returns between FTSE All-Share and Australian All Ordinaries Index for six-month period 31 October–30 April (%)	Difference in summer returns between FTSE All-Share and Australian All Ordinaries Index for six-month period 30 April–31 October (%)
1972	−5.1	−12.2
1973	2.7	3.7
1974	−29.1	−0.3
1975	59.5	−6.5
1976	−1.5	−24.7
1977	51.6	17.9
1978	−11.3	−5.4
1979	18.9	−35.3
1980	−8.0	−15.5
1981	11.9	8.4
1982	23.0	12.5
1983	1.5	−16.6
1984	12.4	1.9
1985	−1.7	−9.6
1986	3.9	−14.9
1987	−0.2	12.7
1988	−7.9	−4.9
1989	18.3	−10.6
1990	9.4	2.6
1991	5.6	−6.7
1992	5.2	11.9
1993	−7.4	−12.9
1994	3.1	−1.8
1995	2.5	8.7
1996	−1.3	0.8
1997	3.3	8.4
1998	9.5	−6.0
1999	3.8	2.9
2000	−3.6	−1.3
2001	−8.9	−13.3
2002	0.5	−13.6
2003	−1.6	1.9
2004	1.5	−8.4
2005	0.2	−0.8
2006	−2.6	−0.6
2007	−8.2	−7.1
2008	6.3	na
Average return	**4.2**	**−3.7**
Up years	22	13
Down years	15	23

Source: Thomson Reuters Datastream

trading strategy 6

Profit from seasonal investing trends in UK and Australia

Global stock markets have a tendency to move in step. For instance, there is a close relationship in the price trends seen in the major indices of the US, European and UK stock markets. So, for the UK market to have outperformed the Australian All Ordinaries Index by such a wide margin during the UK winter and spring months, but underperformed during the UK summer and autumn indicates that some SAD effect could very well be in operation.

One way to profit from this is to simultaneously buy the FTSE 100 Index and to short sell the Australian All Ordinaries Index on 30 October. The FTSE 100 Index accounts for over 75 per cent weighting in the FTSE All-Share Index, so is the best way to track the performance of the UK market. Please note that the size of each trade is identical, so, for every 1 percent move on each market, you will either make or lose the same amount.

This trade is known as a pair trade and is relatively low risk as we are looking to make a higher return by buying the UK market in the winter and spring months than by selling the Australian market during this time. Both the long and short index trades are then closed out on 30 April.

At this point, the trade is reversed by buying the Australian stock market (to benefit from the positive SAD effect during the Australian winter months), while simultaneously short selling the FTSE 100 (which, as we know, underperforms during its summer and autumn). These two new trades are then held open for six months until 31 October, at which point the whole process starts again.

The best way to execute these trades is through two single spread bets with the same spread betting company. In the UK, the leading spread betting firms are IG Index, City Index, Cantor Index, CMC Markets and Capital Spreads. The benefits of carrying out this trade this way are two-fold. First, profits are tax free under the current tax regime in the UK. Second, given that one of the index trades is long (the buy trade) and the other is short (the sell trade) and this gives a reduced risk profile, the amount of cash the spread betting firms will ask you to put up to support the trades will be lower than normal.

" for the UK to have outperformed the Australian market by such a wide margin indicates that some SAD effect could very well be in operation "

Seasonal investing: the summer months

In the same way that we can take advantage of seasonal investing trends in global stock markets, we can also buy and sell sectors when there are clear seasonal patterns in investment returns.

" we can buy and sell sectors when there are clear seasonal patterns in investment returns "

During the summer, defensive sectors – beverages, pharmaceuticals, tobacco, personal care and utilities – outperform the UK market as investors become more risk averse. In the past 25 years, beverages, personal care and tobacco have each boasted average quarterly returns in the second quarter of the year of over 5 per cent against a market average return of 2.1 per cent.

By contrast, more cyclical or growth sectors have traditionally performed poorly in the second quarter. These include construction, general industrials, software, telecoms, electronics and electrical equipment. The poor performance of the construction industry explains why the household goods sector does so badly in the second quarter, as this sector is stuffed full of housebuilders.

" the household goods sector performs badly in the second quarter, as this sector is stuffed full of housebuilders "

It is a similar story going into the third quarter, when we can add the leisure sector to the list of laggards.

trading strategy 7

Seasonality of sectors

Just as we can pair trade two different market indices (by buying one index and simultaneously selling the short the other), we can also pair trade individual sectors of the stock market through spread betting firms. The recommended trading strategy is to buy the five defensive sectors at the end of April. These are beverages, pharmaceuticals, tobacco, personal care and utilities. At the same time, short sell the five cyclical sectors. These are construction, general industrials, software, telecoms, electronics and electrical equipment. Keep these positions open into the traditionally weak month of September and look to take profits in early October.

This type of trade has many benefits. For instance, if the stock market takes an unexpected hit, then the profit on the short trades will help offset any losses on the defensive long positions. However, if the market is flat and the seasonal trends play out – as they have regularly done in the past – this trading strategy has a very good chance of generating a profit on the defensive positions, while profiting from falls in the cyclical sectors.

Seasonal investing: the winter months

❝ in the fourth quarter, technology hardware, electronics and electrical equipment, software and telecoms are the standout gainers **❞**

❝ the one defensive sector that has performed poorly in the past decade is pharmaceuticals **❞**

❝ a pair trade of buying the telecoms sector and simultaneously short selling the pharmaceuticals sector has made an average profit of 8.9 per cent in the past decade **❞**

By the time winter comes, it is time to focus our attention on cyclical sectors as the seasonality process goes into reverse – the defensives now underperforming the growth sectors.

In the fourth quarter, technology hardware, electronics and electrical equipment, software and telecoms are the standout gainers, with telecoms gaining in particular. In fact, the telecom sector has historically risen around 75 per cent of the time in the final quarter of the year, boasting a 3-month return of about 8 per cent in the past couple of decades. However, the electronics and electrical equipment sector is far more volatile, enjoying a higher quarterly return of 11 per cent, but this is countered by the fact that the sector has fallen in this 3-month period no fewer than 10 times since the mid-1980s.

The one defensive sector that has performed poorly in both the fourth and first quarters in the past decade is pharmaceuticals – showing losses, on average, in both periods.

Long-term sector trading

Just as sectors react to effects that boost or hold back their performance at certain times of the year, there is also a trend for sectors that have per-

trading strategy 8

Telecoms and pharmaceuticals

A pair trade of buying the telecoms sector and simultaneously short selling the pharmaceuticals sector between 31 October and 31 January has made an average 3-month profit of 8.9 per cent in the past decade (see Table 5.3). The trade is to buy the telecoms sector through a sector spread bet and short sell the pharmaceuticals sector at the same time.

Please note that the telecoms sector has recently split into mobile telecoms and fixed line telecoms. So, to gain exposure to the *whole* sector, the advice is to buy both telecoms sectors through spread bets. Make sure, though, that for every 1 per cent movement in each market, the amount you will either make or lose is the same as you would with the short sell on the pharmaceuticals sector.

table 5.3 Returns on FTSE All-Share telecoms sector and FTSE 350 pharmaceuticals sector (1998–2008)

Three months to 31 January	FTSE All-Share telecoms return (%)	FTSE 350 pharmaceuticals return (%)	Difference (%)
1998	29.5	26.7	2.8
1999	11.5	11.7	−0.2
2000	30.6	0.1	30.4
2001	−15.6	−2.4	−13.2
2002	−12.9	−14.2	1.2
2003	−1.7	−9.5	7.9
2004	13.8	1.6	12.1
2005	16.3	−2.9	19.1
2006	−10.1	7.5	−17.6
2007	28.2	−8.7	36.9
2008	7.6	−11.0	18.6
Average	8.8	−0.1	8.9

Source: Thomson Reuters Datastream

66 sectors that have performed badly relative to other sectors over a three-year period to reverse this underperformance in the next three years 99

formed badly relative to other sectors over a three-year period to reverse this underperformance in the next three years.

Research by economist Chris Dillow at *Investors Chronicle* (2007) shows a clear negative relationship between the past three-year relative performances of the oil, banks, pharmaceuticals and retailing sectors and their subsequent three-year returns relative to one another. The data sample he used was from a 30-year period from 1977 to 2007 (see Table 5.4).

table 5.4   Sector ratios and subsequent three-year relative returns (monthly data sample, 1977–2007)

Sectors	Correlation	R-squared
Oil/banks	−0.36	13.1
Oil/pharmaceuticals	−0.42	17.8
Oil/retailers	−0.46	21.2
Oil/All-Share	−0.49	24.0
Banks/pharmaceuticals	−0.49	24.0
Banks/retailers	−0.21	4.4
Banks/All-Share	−0.19	3.6
Pharmaceuticals/retailers	−0.43	18.4
Pharmaceuticals/All-Share	−0.50	25.0
Retailers/All-Share	−0.57	33.0

Source: *Investors Chronicle*

Noting that UK banks were trading at a 12-year low relative to oil stocks, Mr Dillow observed that, when oil stocks were highly valued relative to banks – for instance, in 1980, 1985 or 1991 – they subsequently under-performed banks in the following three years. When the oil majors were rated low relative to banks – 1984, 1994 and 1999 – this was a precursor to subsequent relative outperformance. This is best illustrated by means of Figure 5.1.

❝ oil stocks were highly valued relative to banks – for instance, in 1980, 1985 or 1991 – they subsequently underperformed banks in the following three years ❞

The fact that the laggards start to outperform after three years is really no surprise as investors have a habit of overreacting to bad news, pushing shares down. In the same way, they get carried away with a good news story, sending stocks overshoot-ing fair value to the upside. As a result, the laggards become underpriced, while the outper-formers become overpriced. However, mean reversion back towards the average historic earnings multiples for each sector eventually kicks in, helping the laggards to start outperforming. On a three-year timeframe, this pattern seems to work rather well.

Low valuations can also indicate risk aversion by investors who, in the case of the banking sector in 2008, were wary of their balance sheet risk following hefty losses incurred on US sub-prime mortgages and rising mortgage arrears in the UK. Equally, investors may have been very com-

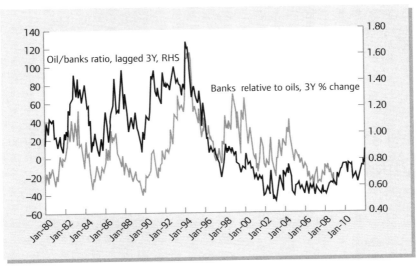

figure 5.1 Banks' performance relative to oil stocks since 1980

❝❝ low valuations can also indicate risk aversion by investors who, in the case of the banking sector in 2008, were wary of their balance sheet risk following hefty losses incurred on US sub-prime mortgages ❞❞

fortable about holding oil stocks, given that record oil prices of $147 a barrel reached in July 2008 underpinned profits for the oil majors. So, in a sense, investors needed higher future returns from banking stocks to compensate for this perceived higher risk, while they were willing to accept lower returns from oil stocks with their lower perceived risks. These risk characteristics are another reason for laggards eventually outperforming the outperformers.

trading strategy 9

Mean reversion

Mean reversion of relative sector valuations has worked well in the past and should continue to do so in the future. It is therefore worth monitoring the outperformance of the four major stock market sectors – oil, banks, pharmaceuticals and retailing. When one sector is at a multi-year low relative to one of the three others and has significantly underperformed that sector in the past three years, then that is a cue to take out a sector long spread bet on the laggard sector and, simultaneously, short sell the outperforming sector. True, this trade is one for the long-term, but, if history is any guide, it will generate long-term profits.

chapter

6

Federal Reserve's
rate-cutting cycles

'Don't fight the Federal Reserve' is one of Wall Street's famous mantras. The theory goes that stocks do well during interest rate-cutting cycles and less so when interest rates are on the rise. Coupled with this is the fact that the Federal Reserve is charged with keeping a watch over both economic growth and monetary conditions, making many investors believe that the US central bank has great power over the stock market. So, are investors wise in thinking like this or is there a smarter way to profit from rate-cutting cycles?

Federal Reserve rate-cutting cycles

Let's consider how the S&P 500 Index has performed in the 13 interest rate-cutting cycles of the past 6 decades. The start of the cycle is the date when the Federal Reserve funds' rate is first cut and the end is when the period of monetary easing is deemed over, signalled by a rise in the Federal Reserve funds rate. The findings are very informative (see Table 6.1).

❝ the best of the gains have actually been enjoyed in the period between the final rate cut and when the Federal Reserve raises rates ❞

Over this 54-year period, these monetary cutting cycles have lasted 24 months, on average (see final column in Table 6.1) and have been accompanied by an average rise in the S&P 500 of 33 per cent (see the penultimate column). It's worth noting, though, that, as the average rise in the

table 6.1 S&P 500's performance during Federal Reserve easing cycles since 1954

Cycle start date (first rate cut)	Date of last rate cut	Cycle end date	Total cuts in cycle	Total gain/loss in S&P 500 between first and last rate cut (%)	Total gain/loss in S&P 500 in cycle (%)	Period from first cut to end of cycle (months)
05/02/1954	19/04/1954	14/04/1955	2	6%	44%	14
15/11/1957	18/04/1958	11/09/1958	4	6%	20%	10
10/06/1960	12/08/1960	16/07/1963	2	-2%	19%	37
13/11/1970	19/02/1971	15/07/1971	5	16%	19%	8
19/11/1971	17/12/1971	12/01/1973	2	9%	30%	14
09/12/1974	22/11/1976	30/08/1977	7	56%	47%	33
30/05/1980	28/07/1980	25/09/1980	3	9%	16%	4
02/11/1981	15/12/1982	06/04/1984	9	9%	25%	29
21/11/1984	21/08/1986	03/09/1987	7	52%	95%	34
06/06/1989	04/09/1992	03/02/1994	24	29%	48%	56
06/07/1995	31/01/1996	24/03/1997	3	15%	43%	20
29/09/1998	17/11/1998	29/06/1999	3	9%	29%	9
03/01/2001	25/06/2003	29/06/2004	13	-28%	-16%	42
18/09/2007	08/10/2008*	TBD	7	-33%	TBD	TBD
Average			6	14%**	33%	24

* Last rate cut in current cycle

** Average return for completed cycles

Source: Charles Schwab

Index is 14.3 per cent between the date of the first interest rate cut and the final one, the best of the gains have actually been enjoyed in the period between the final rate cut and when the Federal Reserve signals the start of the monetary tightening cycle by raising rates. In fact, the S&P 500 has continued to rise after the final rate cut in all bar 1 of the past 13 completed rate-cutting cycles (see Table 6.2), posting an average gain of 15.7 per cent. The period from last rate cut to the start of the tightening cycle has averaged 12 months since 1954.

So, the strategy of buying the S&P 500 Index once the Federal Reserve has signalled the end of the interest rate-cutting cycle and keeping this position open until the first rate rise, has proved a passport to prosperity in the past six decades. Not only has the 15.7 per cent gain in the Index

table 6.2   S&P 500's performance during Federal Reserve easing cycles since 1954

Date of last rate cut	Cycle end date	Total cuts in cycle	Total gain/loss in S&P 500 between last rate cut and end of cycle (%)	Period from last rate cut and start of tightening cycle (months)
19/04/1954	14/04/1955	2	36%	12
18/04/1958	11/09/1958	4	13%	5
12/08/1960	16/07/1963	2	21%	35
19/02/1971	15/07/1971	5	3%	5
17/12/1971	12/01/1973	2	19%	13
22/11/1976	30/08/1977	7	−6%	9
28/07/1980	25/09/1980	3	6%	2
15/12/1982	06/04/1984	9	15%	16
21/08/1986	03/09/1987	7	28%	13
04/09/1992	03/02/1994	24	15%	17
31/01/1996	24/03/1997	3	24%	14
17/11/1998	29/06/1999	3	18%	7
25/06/2003	29/06/2004	13	17%	12
08/10/2008*	TBD	7	TBD	TBD
Average		6	16%	12

* Last rate cut to date in current cycle

Source: Charles Schwab

❝ the strategy of buying the S&P 500 Index once the Federal Reserve has signalled the end of the interest rate-cutting cycle and keeping this position open until the first rate rise, has proved a passport to prosperity ❞

❝ you would have enjoyed bumper profits if you had bought the S&P 500 Index on the last rate cut in June 2003 as it was not until June 2004 that monetary policy started to tighten again ❞

over the average 12-month period from the last rate cut been significantly above the long-term average return from the S&P 500 Index, but the strategy has only failed to work once since 1954. Even then, in 1976–1997, the loss was modest, at 6 per cent. Remember, too, since 1980, that this strategy has had a 100 per cent track record, with the market rising every time between the date of the last rate cut and when the Federal Reserve starts to raise interest rates.

Moreover, this buy-on-the-last-rate-cut strategy would have helped avoid the deep losses investors suffered during the painful US equity bear market running between March 2000 and October 2002, which coincided with the rate-cutting cycle that started in January 2001. This was because the last rate cut took place in June 2003 – three months after the bear market had ended. In fact, you would have enjoyed bumper profits if you had bought the S&P 500 Index on the last rate cut in June 2003 as it was not until June 2004 that monetary policy started to tighten again. In that 12-month period, the S&P 500 Index rose 17 per cent, underpinned by improving economic conditions and rising corporate profits.

Reasons for the 'buy-on-the-last-rate-cut' phenomenon

It's easy to understand why this phenomenon works as stocks will start to rise in advance of the economic recovery as investors bet that the easing

❝ when the Federal Reserve signals that the rate-cutting cycle has gone far enough it is a sign that the bank believes that the recovery is well on its way ❞

of monetary policy will give the economy a big enough boost to pull it out of the slowdown or recession. So, when the Federal Reserve finally signals that the rate-cutting cycle has gone far enough and the period of monetary easing is over, it is a sign that the US's central bank believes that the recovery in the economy is well on its way. In turn, this signal underpins investors' confidence and they start buying equities more aggressively.

> **“** buying on the final rate cut and keeping the position open until rates start to rise again would have generated a profit of 15.7 per cent since 1954 **”**

Remember, too, that the monetary easing will have a positive and lagged impact on corporate earnings as it takes time for the full impact of rate cuts to feed through the system. As the stock market is a pretty efficient, forward-looking discount mechanism, this explains why stocks generally bottom out between four and six months before US recessions end in anticipation of the upturn.

trading strategy 10

Buy-on-the-last-rate-cut strategy

If you are relying on cuts in the Federal Reserve funds rate alone, then buying the S&P 500 Index after the final rate cut – which is generally signalled as such by the wording of the statement accompanying the Federal Reserve Open Market Committee's rate decision – has proved a sound strategy. Buying on the final rate cut and keeping the position open until rates start to rise again would have generated a profit of 15.7 per cent, on average, since 1954, with all bar one of the 13 cycles showing a profit.

One way to benefit from the buy-on-the-last-rate-cut trading strategy is to buy an ETF listed on the London Stock Exchange that tracks the performance of the S&P 500 Index, such as Barclays: Shares (TIDM:IUSA). ETFs are traded in exactly the same way as ordinary shares.

Fosback and the Federal Reserve

Another way to look at the rate-cutting cycle is to consider what happens to the stock market in the *early* part of the cycle and, specifically, after the Federal Reserve lowers one of its three main key policy variables: discount rate, reserve requirement or margin requirement.

Norman Fosback, former head of the Institute for Econometric Research, discovered that, when the Federal Reserve lowers any one of these three variables twice in a row, having previously raised rates, this is a great leading indicator of strong future returns on US equity markets. In fact, in the past five decades, the S&P 500 has risen, on average, 4 per cent in the first 20 calendar days following the second rate cut and, after 3 months, it has been 11 per cent ahead and, after a year, up by almost 30 per cent (Wagner, 2007).

In September 2007, Hans Wagner, of Tradingmarketsonline.com, updated Fosback's theory by analysing how the US stock market performed in the 12-month period after the second rate cut during each easing cycle since 1954 (see Table 6.3).

table 6.3 Performance of S&P 500 following two rate cuts since 1954

Signal No.	Date of signal (second time rate was lowered)	S&P 500 maximum percentage gain within a year	S&P 500 maximum percentage loss within a year
1	16 April 1954	36%	−1%
2	24 January 1958	34%	−3%
3	12 August 1960	20%	−7%
4	10 July 1962	24%	−6%
5	4 December 1970	17%	0%
6	6 December 1971	22%	0%
7	9 January 1975	34%	−1%
8	12 June 1980	22%	−1%
9	3 December 1981	31%	−3%
10	22 November 1983	96%	−11%
11	29 October 1989	39%	−16%
12	19 December 1995	150%	−2%
13	31 January 2001	0%	−39%
14	18 September 2007	7%	−18%
Average		**38%**	**−8%**

Source: Trading Online Markets LLC

The results are pretty astonishing. First, it can be seen that the S&P 500 reacts very favourably from the date of the second rate cut. Indeed, taking the highs in the Index during the 12-month period that followed the second rate cut, on average, the S&P 500 has risen by 38 per cent to these peaks. True, it would have taken a Midas touch to bank profits every time at these highs and the index was also down at some point in most of these 12-month periods (see the final column), but investors riding out these short-term losses would have been rewarded with bumper gains in 12 of the 14 cycles.

The problem with this 'buy on the second rate cut strategy', however, is the poor stock market return following the January 2001 rate cuts, which was in the midst of the March 2000 to October 2002 US equity bear market. In fact, the 39 per cent fall in the market in the 12 months from January 2001 would have been catastrophic. It was a similar story in the bear market of 2007/2008 when stocks also fell heavily during the interest rate-cutting cycle that started in September 2007.

ⅭⅭ there is a reason for the 'buy-on-the-second-rate-cut' strategy failing to work in 2001 and 2007: equity valuations and the yield curve 🟥🟥

Fortunately, there is a reason for the 'buy-on-the-second-rate-cut' strategy failing to work in 2001 and 2007: equity valuations and the yield curve. By taking into consideration these two variables, we can greatly mitigate the risk of losing money by calculating when it is safe to buy early in the rate-cutting cycle.

Monetary easing, equity valuations and the US yield curve

Liz Ann Sonders (2008), Senior Vice President and Chief Investment Strategist at Charles Schwab Stockbrokers, notes that, 'rate cuts tend to work better for stocks when they commence after a major stock market shock (the investment house defines this as a fall in the S&P 500 Index of 15 per cent), when inflation and the price environment is relatively benign and corporate profits are not contracting.' The data seems to back her up.

ⅭⅭ rate cuts tend to work better for stocks when they commence after a major stock market shock 🟥🟥

Equity valuations

First, the bumper returns that have been generated by buying the S&P 500 Index on the second rate cut have one thing in common – low valuations. For instance, investors had suffered significant losses by the end of 1974, following a brutal 21-month bear market that had wiped 46 per cent off share prices. So, the 56 per cent gain in the Index between the first and last cuts in that cycle were also being driven by low valuations as the US market was trading on less than eight times earnings when rates were first cut.

Fast forward to the early 1980s and the story was pretty similar, with stocks trading well below ten times earnings when the Federal Reserve started to cut rates in the two cycles in 1980 and 1981. However, in January 2001, following the dot.com boom, valuations were certainly *not* low, even though the earnings multiple of the S&P 500 had tumbled from its March 2000 dot.com peak of 30.5 to 26.4 nine months later. By the same token, the S&P 500 Index was still trading on 19.4 times historic earnings in September 2007. So was the market too expensive to rise at the start of the rate-cutting cycle in January 2001 and September 2007?

❝ when valuations are too rich at the start of the rate-cutting cycle subsequent returns on the S&P 500 Index have been very poor indeed ❞

Research from US Investment house Hussman Funds seems to suggest that this was the case (Hester, 2007). Hussman showed that, when the market's price to peak earnings (PE) multiple has been below 15 during rate-cutting cycles, the first rate cut has been followed, on average, by a gain in the S&P 500 of over 25 per cent in both the following 12- and 18-month periods. However, when valuations are too rich at the start of the rate-cutting cycle (when the PE ratio is above 17), Hussman found that the subsequent returns on the S&P 500 Index have been very poor indeed, averaging only around 6 per cent in the following 12 and 18 months.

The shape of the US yield curve

Aside from the valuation of the stock market at the start of the rate-cutting cycle, Hussman found another significant variable that has a great impact on subsequent equity market returns: the slope of the US yield curve. When long-term rates (yields on 10-year US Treasury bonds) are significantly higher than short-term rates (yields on 90-day Treasury bills), this leads to a steep yield curve with positive implications for economic growth. By contrast, an inverted yield curve has proved a very good warning sign over the years that the economy is set for a slowdown or recession.

❝ an inverted yield curve has proved a very good warning sign over the years that the economy is set for a slowdown or recession ❞

So, combining the shape of the yield curve at the start of the rate-cutting cycle with the valuation of the market, Hussman was able to break down the stock market's performance following rate cuts into four distinct bands (see Figure 6.1). Namely, when the PE ratio is either below 15 or above 17 and the yield curve is either inverted or upward sloping.

The results shown in Figure 6.1 confirm that when the period of monetary easing started when valuations were low (the PE ratio on the S&P 500 was below 15), then, irrespective of the slope of the yield curve, the stock market was significantly higher 6, 12 and 18 months after the first cut.

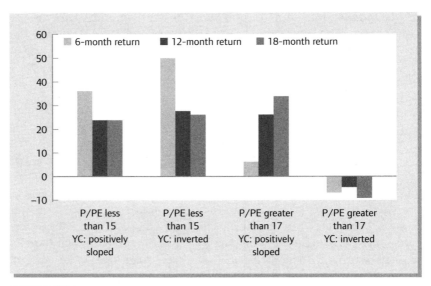

Source: Hussman Funds

figure 6.1   Performance of S&P 500 following two rate cuts since 1954

Equally, even a highly rated market managed to post decent returns in monetary easing cycles, but only if the yield curve was upward-sloping.

Hussman also found, however, that the S&P 500 performed poorly when it was highly rated at the start of the cycle (the PE ratio on the S&P 500 was above 17) and the yield curve was inverted, with the Index dropping by an average of 4.4 per cent over the subsequent 12 months.

So, by combining the findings of Fosback and Hussman, we can hone in on an investment strategy to play the monetary easing cycle in its early stages.

trading strategy 11

Buy-on-the-second-rate-cut strategy

Irrespective of the shape of the yield curve, it is worth buying the S&P 500 on the second rate cut in an interest rate-cutting cycle on a 6- to 12-month timeframe, but only if the stock market is lowly rated (a PE ratio of below 15) to start with. Please note that the second cut is when the Federal Reserve lowers one of its three main key policy variables – discount rate, reserve requirement or margin requirement.

Time to be patient

If the market is highly rated (a PE ratio of above 17) and the yield curve is upward-sloping, the best returns have historically been generated between 6 and 18 months after the first rate cut, so a waiting brief is recommended with a view to buying the S&P 500 Index some time after six months following the second rate cut.

Heed the shape of the yield curve

An inverted yield curve coupled with a high valuation (a PE ratio of above 17 – as was the case in 2001 and 2007) is a bad omen for the performance of the stock market on all three timeframes following the cuts – 6, 12 and 18 months. The buy-on-the-second-rate-cut strategy is the optimum choice here, but with the proviso that you should look to lock in profits at some point between 20 calendar days and 3 months after the second rate cut as the odds are heavily stacked that the rally will peter out soon thereafter.

In fact, that is exactly what happened in the autumn of 2007, with the S&P 500 Index rising from 1445 on 18 September 2007 (the date the Federal Reserve cut its Federal Funds rate having previously lowered the discount rate (the rate banks can borrow from the central bank) to a record high of 1576 on 11 October 2007. That was a rise of 9 per cent in less than a month. However, six months later, on 17 March 2008, in the aftermath of the near collapse of US investment bank Bear Sterns, the Index had plunged to 1258 – a drop of 21 per cent from that all-time high. By mid-October 2008, the S&P 500 had fallen 43 per cent drop from that autumn all-time high.

It is no coincidence that the inverted yield curve had been warning of an economic slowdown (short-term rates were above long-term rates) and equity valuations were not cheap either. Remember, in September 2007, the Index was trading on 19.4 times earnings. The stock market is clearly less forgiving of economic slowdowns if valuations are not overinflated to start with (see next page on bond yields for further information).

❝ ❝ the stock market is clearly less forgiving of economic slowdowns if valuations are not overinflated to start with ❞ ❞

Bond yields

Traditionally, bond yields and equities have been positively correlated in low-interest rate environments as both respond to changes in the economic climate by moving in the same direction. That is why falling inflation in the 1980s and 1990s produced a great tailwind for bonds, the prices of which rose and yields fell to reflect the more benign inflationary backdrop. In turn, this also gave a great boost to stock markets, since earnings yields (the inverse of the earnings multiple) became relatively more attractive as bond yields fell. The further bond yields fall, however – reflecting reduced inflationary risk – the more sensitive stock prices are to changes in economic growth rather than inflation.

In part, this is perhaps why the deteriorating economic backdrop in the early 2000s led to such a savage bear market, as stock prices were not only falling from record high valuations but also, given the low bond yields, equity markets were far more sensitive than usual to fluctuations in the economy. That is another reason why rate-cutting cycles – during periods when inflation and bond yields have been low, and stock markets have been highly valued – have produced such miserable returns for equity investors.

7

US presidential cycle

Like clockwork, US citizens go to the polls every four years. This is in stark contrast to the UK electoral process, where endless governments have faced the dilemma of whether to call an early election or delay the day of reckoning to the last minute.

The reason for the predictability of the US electoral process is that election day is set by law, falling on the first Tuesday following the first Monday of November. As a result, the first Tuesday will always fall between 2 and 8 November. Moreover, presidential elections are always held in years divisible by four, so the last US election took place on 4 November 2008.

❝ this consistency and predictability in the US election process enables successive governments to try and influence both monetary and fiscal policy ahead of the election ❞

That's not the only difference between the two electoral systems. Whereas in the UK the incumbent prime minister has to make a hasty exit from 10 Downing Street if the result is not in his or her favour, the US approach is less hurried. Inauguration day – the day on which a US president is sworn in and takes office – is fixed in statute in accordance with the twentieth amendment to the United States' constitution. Since the beginning of Franklin Roosevelt's second term in office in 1937, both the president and vice-president's terms start at noon on 20 January following the US presidential elections the previous November.

US fiscal and monetary policy

It is this consistency and predictability in the US election process that enables successive governments to try and influence both monetary and fiscal policy ahead of the election in an attempt to sway voters. After all, it is in the obvious interest of the incumbent administration to make sure voter approval is maximised ahead of going to the ballot boxes. With this in mind, the executive branch of the government can time the implementation of fiscal policy (either through changes to taxation or spending plans) in order to give a boost to the economy in the run-up to an election and make people more prosperous.

> **"the government can time the implementation of fiscal policy ... to give a boost to the economy in the run-up to an election and make people more prosperous"**

Equally, there is some merit in the argument that the government has an interest in trying to influence monetary policy, too, by pressurising the US's central bank, the Federal Reserve, to ease monetary conditions. This can be done through lower interest rates and increases in the money supply to give a further boost to the economy and, in so doing, give voters that feel-good factor. In reality, it is debatable and very subjective how much the executive branch of the US administration can influence monetary policy.

That said, right on cue, the cuts in US interest rates from the autumn of 2007, coupled with the attempts of the Federal Reserve to boost liquidity in distressed financial money and bond markets – in response to a rapidly slowing US economy and the fall-out from the 2007 sub-prime mortgage crisis – is exactly the easing of monetary policy that the Bush administration would have wanted ahead of the November 2008 election. It is no surprise either that the Bush government rushed through a fiscal package of measures, in election year, to ease the financial problems of embattled consumers and mortgage holders.

> **"investors are more likely to aggressively buy equities in the years running up to an election, if anything goes wrong, the government and Federal Reserve will come to the rescue"**

In turn, this raises another major issue: moral hazard. Namely, if investors realise, in the run-up to an election, that the government and the Federal Reserve are more inclined to operate in this fashion, then it gives them greater confidence. That is logical as the economic measures being implemented ahead of the election will benefit companies, too, helping improve corporate profits. In turn, investors are more likely to aggressively buy equities in the years running up to an election, safe in the knowledge that, if anything goes wrong, the government and Federal Reserve will come to the rescue.

Assuming that the gamble by the government pays off, the story is rather different following the election. That's because the pre-election tax cuts and spending spree will have weakened the public finances and, as a result, the process goes into reverse as the mini-boom, fuelled by the economic stimulus, starts to wear off. In the circumstances, it would be rational for the US stock market to react accordingly to the mini-boom and economic retrenchment by performing less well in the two years following an election, only to get a boost again come the pre-election and election year.

❝ it would be rational for the US stock market to react accordingly to the mini-boom and economic retrenchment by performing less well in the two years following an election ❞

So, does the actual performance of the US equity market during the four-year presidential term support the theory of a mini-boom followed by a period of economic retrenchment?

The impact of presidential elections on the US stock market

Whether you believe that there is manipulation over fiscal and monetary policy ahead of the election or not, what can't be doubted is that the stock market behaves as if there is.

First, let's consider the return on the US equity market for the four-year presidential cycle from 1965 to 2007 (see Tables 7.1a–d). The first year of the cycle starts on 1 January following the election in November and the final year is the year of the next election. The returns in the tables give the performance of the Dow Jones Industrial Average Index for each calendar year in turn.

❝ the boost to the economy in the run-up to the election starts to wear off pretty quickly after the new president has taken office ❞

The results are pretty astonishing. In the first and second years of the cycle (Tables 7.1a and 7.1b), the average annual return over the past 11 cycles has been a pitiful 3.3 per cent and 1 per cent, respectively, with as many down years as up years. This is in keeping with the theory that the boost to the economy in the run-up to the election starts to wear off pretty quickly after the new president has taken office. In effect, investors get a bout of the post-election blues.

table 7.1a   Performance of US market in first year of US presidential cycles since 1965

Year	Performance of Dow Jones Industrial Average in calendar year
1965	10.9
1969	−15.2
1973	−16.6
1977	−17.3
1981	−9.2
1985	27.7
1989	27.0
1993	13.7
1997	22.6
2001	−7.1
2005	−0.6
Average annual return	**3.3**
Up years	5
Down years	6

Source: Thomson Reuters Datastream

table 7.1b   Performance of US market in second year of US presidential cycles since 1965

Year	Performance of Dow Jones Industrial Average in calendar year
1966	−18.9
1970	4.8
1974	−27.6
1978	−3.2
1982	19.6
1986	22.6
1990	−4.3
1994	2.1
1998	16.1
2002	−16.8
2006	16.3
Average annual return	**1.0**
Up years	6
Down years	5

Source: Thomson Reuters Datastream

" " in the third year of the cycle, the US stock market has a 100 per cent record, with 11 up cycles out of 11, posting an average annual gain of 17.9 per cent " "

In the third year of the cycle (see Table 7.1c) however, the US stock market has a 100 per cent record, with 11 up cycles out of 11, posting an average annual gain of 17.9 per cent. This trend has a habit of continuing into election year (see Table 7.1d), when the average rise in the Dow has been 8.7 per cent, with 8 up years out of the past 10.

table 7.1c Performance of US market in third year of US presidential cycles since 1965

Year	Performance of Dow Jones Industrial Average in calendar year
1967	15.2
1971	6.1
1975	38.3
1979	4.2
1983	20.3
1987	2.3
1991	20.3
1995	33.5
1999	25.2
2003	25.3
2007	6.4
Average annual return	**17.9**
Up years	11
Down years	0

Source: Thomson Reuters Datastream

table 7.1d Performance of US market in fourth year of US presidential cycles since 1965

Year	Performance of Dow Jones Industrial Average in calendar year
1968	4.3
1972	14.6
1976	17.9
1980	14.9
1984	−3.7
1988	11.9
1992	4.2
1996	26.0
2000	−6.2
2004	3.2
Average annual return	**8.7**
Up years	8
Down years	2

Source: Thomson Reuters Datastream

trading strategy 14

A New (third) Year Dow Jones Industrial Average Index tracker

The optimum trading strategy, and one with a 100 per cent track record, is to buy a Dow Jones Industrial Average Index tracker on the 1 January in the third year of the presidential cycle and keep the position open until the end of the year to capture the average 17.9 per cent annual gain.

If you want to benefit from this trend, ETFs listed on the London Stock Exchange that track the performance of the Dow Jones Industrial Average include those issued by Lyxor, a wholly owned subsidiary of Société Générale (TIDM: LIND, issued in sterling, and TIDM: LINU, issued in US dollars). Please note that ETFs can be bought or sold through stockbrokers in the same way as shares in any listed company.

Moreover, the chances of losing money in the fourth year has been minimal in the past four decades, as the 2 down election years in the past 10 cycles – 1984 and 2000 – only showed falls of 3.7 per cent and 6.2 per cent, respectively. That's reason enough to stay invested through the election year itself. However, there is an even smarter way to make even bigger gains.

> **"** the optimum trading strategy, and one with a 100 per cent track record, is to buy a Dow Jones Industrial Average Index tracker on the 1 January of the third year and keep the position open until the end of the year **"**

The US presidential cycle and avoiding bear markets

Research from Dr Marshall Nickles (2004), an economics professor at California's Pepperdine University's Graziadio School of Business and Management, shows that we can fine-tune our investment strategy to improve the odds of generating higher returns during the four-year cycle.

By looking at all the bull and bear markets in the US since 1942, Dr Nickles analysed the performance of the S&P 500 Index with the aim of seeing if there was a trend in the timing of bear market lows. The results are astonishing (see Table 7.2), with bear markets (defined by Dr Nickles as a period where prices drop by at least 15 per cent over a period of 1–3 years) showing a clear tendency to bottom out in the second year of the US presidential cycle (12 times out of the past 16 cycles) or the first year (3 times out of the past 16 cycles).

table 7.2 Presidential elections and market troughs

Presidential term	Month and year of market bottom trough	Year during presidential term when market bottomed
1942–1944	April 1942	2nd
1945–1948	October 1946	2nd
1949–1952	June 1949	1st
1953–1956	September 1953	1st
1957–1960	October 1957	1st
1961–1964	June 1962	2nd
1965–1968	October 1966	2nd
1969–1972	May 1970	2nd
1973–1976	October 1974	2nd
1977–1980	March 1978	2nd
1981–1984	August 1982	2nd
1985–1988	December 1987	3rd
1989–1992	October 1990	2nd
1993–1996	April 1994	2nd
1997 –2000	August 1998	2nd
2001–2004	October 2002	2nd
		Average = 22.5 months into presidential term

Source: Marshall D. Nickles, EdD, 'Presidential Elections and Stock Market Cycles,' 2004, Graziadio Business Report, Pepperdine University, http://gbr.pepperdine.edu/043/stocks.html

> **❝the results are astonishing with bear markets showing a clear tendency to bottom out in the second year of the US presidential cycle or the first year❞**

Next comes the really smart bit. By combining the political and the stock market peak-to-trough cycles, we can home in on the best time to take advantage of both. With this in mind, Dr Nickles found that the optimum time to buy the S&P 500 Index tracker is on 1 October in the second year of the presidential term and then to hold this position open until the end of December in the fourth year. In fact, since the 1952 election – a 56-year period, covering the past 14 presidential cycles – this strategy has generated an incredible average return of 40 per cent over each 27-month period (see Table 7.3).

Most important of all, there were no down years as this system reduces the risk of encountering a bear market, which we know from Table 7.2 is most likely to bottom out in the first or second years of the political cycle. By contrast, the market performs poorly during the first 21 months

table 7.3   Investment strategies over US presidential term (1952–2004)

Year of presidential election	Percentage change in S&P 500 from 1 October of second year of presidential term through to 31 December of election year
1952	35
1956	45
1960	16
1964	52
1968	39
1972	40
1976	70
1980	32
1984	37
1988	19
1992	38
1996	60
2000	34
2004	49
Average return	**40**
Up years	14
Down years	0

Source: Marshall D. Nickles, EdD, 'Presidential Elections and Stock Market Cycles,' 2004, Graziadio Business Report, Pepperdine University, http://gbr.pepperdine.edu/043/stocks.html

「「 the optimum time to buy the S&P 500 Index tracker is on 1 October in the second year of the presidential term and then hold this position open until the end of December in the fourth year 」」

of the new Presidential term (see Table 7.4) with the S&P 500 Index posting an average return of just 8 per cent from 1 January of the first year through to the end of September of the second year since 1952.

Reasons for this phenomenon

So why does a trading strategy of buying the S&P 500 on 1 October of the second year of the presidential term and holding this position open until after the next election work every time? First, stock markets have a habit of heading southwards when risk aversion rises – and, in particular, when investors start to fret over the risk to corporate profitability from a deteriorating economic backdrop. The odds of this happening in the pre-election year or election year are much reduced, given that the government has a vested interest in giving the economy a boost (which enhances the outlook for corporate profits, too)

table 7.4 Investment strategies over US presidential term (1952–2004)

Year of presidential election	Percentage change in S&P 500 from 1 January of inaugural year through to 30 September of second year of presidential term
1952	22
1956	8
1960	−2
1964	−9
1968	−19
1972	−47
1976	−4
1980	−12
1984	40
1988	11
1992	7
1996	42
2000	−36
2004	10
Average return	8
Up years	7
Down years	7

Source: Marshall D. Nickles, EdD, 'Presidential Elections and Stock Market Cycles,' 2004, Graziadio Business Report, Pepperdine University, http://gbr.pepperdine.edu/043/stocks.html

❝ stock markets have a habit of heading southwards when risk aversion rises and investors fret over the risk to corporate profitability from a deteriorating economic backdrop ❞

to improve its chances of re-election. However, after the election, the impact of tighter fiscal policy – and potentially tighter monetary policy if there is a need for the Federal Reserve to combat inflationary pressures – mean that investors are more likely to start worrying about the outlook for company profits.

Second, Dr Nickles found that major market peak-to-trough cycles have a habit of making V-shaped bottoms after prices have fallen over 10 per cent and, in the main, by over 20 per cent. These bear markets also have a tendency to bottom out in the first and second years of the US presidential cycle before bouncing back strongly.

The subsequent recovery in equity prices is then helped along by a strong economic stimulus, implemented by government in an attempt to stave off the chances of a politically unpopular economic slowdown/recession. Investors react to these measures by buying shares aggressively in advance of the anticipated economic recovery. This could also explain why, in election years, the S&P 500 Index has risen between 1 June and 31 December in no fewer than 13 of the past 14 US presidential terms (with an average gain of 7.2 per cent). The one exception was in 2000,

❝ in election years, the S&P 500 Index has risen between 1 June and 31 December in no fewer than 13 of the past 14 US presidential terms ❞

when the Index fell by 7.1 per cent in this 7-month period. There was a justifiable reason for this: uncertainty over the election result after the Democratic Party requested a manual recount of the hotly contested Florida vote.

In fact, the result of the 2000 presidential election was not declared for a further 36 days after election day itself, creating great uncertainty in the financial markets. In the event, the US Supreme Court prevented the Democratic party's bid for a recount and George Bush was elected President.

trading strategy 15

Buy a S&P 500 Index tracker on 1 October, second year

A system that has had no down years for the 14 presidential cycles and generated a profit of 40 per cent, on average, in each of the 27-month periods – from 1 October of the second year of the presidential term through to 31 December of election year – makes this one of the most profitable trades going. For the record, the last US presidential election was on 4 November 2008, the new president takes office on 20 January 2009 and the recommended trade is to buy a S&P 500 Index tracker on 1 October 2010 and keep the position open until 31 December 2012 following the next election in November 2012.

If you want to benefit from this trend, one way to do so is by buying an ETF listed on the London Stock Exchange. ETFs that track the performance of the S&P 500 Index include those issued by Barclays iShares (TIDM: IUSA).

The UK stock market and the US presidential cycle

Unbelievably, there is a third way to profit from the presidential cycle and it also has a 100 per cent track record.

> **unbelievably, there is a third way to profit from the presidential cycle and it also has a 100 per cent track record, in the past four decades, the FTSE All-Share Index has never fallen in the third year of the cycle**

Let's consider the performance of the FTSE All-Share Index between 1965 and 2007 – a period that covers the last 11 US presidential cycles (see Tables 7.5a–d). Not surprisingly, given the strong relationship between the price performances of global equity markets, the UK stock market follows a similar pattern to that of the US markets by performing very poorly in the second year of the US presidential term (see Table 7.5b: average loss of 4.5 per cent), but rallying strongly in the third and fourth years. In fact, in the past four decades, the FTSE All-Share Index has never fallen in the third year of the cycle (see Table 7.5c). Moreover, the average gain of 28.4 per cent in the third year is a full 10 percentage points higher than the return generated on the Dow Jones Industrial Average in the third year of the cycle. So, the lesson is, buy an index tracker in the UK stock market at the start of the third year of the US presidential cycle.

> **the return in the fourth year has been a very healthy 14 per cent in the past 10 cycles with only 2 down years since 1968**

It gets better, too, as the return in the fourth year has been a very healthy 14 per cent in the past 10 cycles (see Table 7.5d), with only 2 down years since 1968. That compares very favourably with the US market, which posted an average gain of 8.7 per cent in the fourth year in the same period.

table 7.5a   Performance of UK market in first year of US presidential cycles since 1965

Year	Performance of FTSE All-Share Index in calendar year
1965	6.7
1969	−15.2
1973	−31.4
1977	41.2
1981	7.2
1985	15.2
1989	30.0
1993	23.4
1997	19.7
2001	−15.4
2005	18.1
Average annual return	**9.0**
Up years	8
Down years	3

Source: Thomson Reuters Datastream

table 7.5b   Performance of UK market in second year of US presidential cycles since 1965

Year	Performance of FTSE All-Share Index in calendar year
1966	−9.3
1970	−7.5
1974	−55.3
1978	2.7
1982	22.1
1986	22.3
1990	−14.3
1994	−9.6
1998	10.9
2002	−25.0
2006	13.2
Average annual return	**−4.5**
Up years	5
Down years	6

Source: Thomson Reuters Datastream

table 7.5c Performance of UK market in third year of US presidential cycles since 1965

Year	Performance of FTSE All-Share Index in calendar year
1967	29.0
1971	41.9
1975	136.3
1979	4.4
1983	23.1
1987	4.2
1991	15.1
1995	18.5
1999	21.3
2003	16.6
2007	2.0
Average annual return	28.4
Up years	11
Down years	0

Source: Thomson Reuters Datastream

table 7.5d Performance of UK market in fourth year of US presidential cycles since 1965

Year	Performance of FTSE All-Share Index in calendar year
1968	43.4
1972	12.8
1976	−3.9
1980	27.2
1984	26.0
1988	6.5
1992	14.8
1996	11.7
2000	−8.0
2004	9.2
Average annual return	14.0
Up years	8
Down years	2

Source: Thomson Reuters Datastream

So not only does the UK market easily outperform the US market in the fourth year of the cycle, but the losses incurred in the down years (3.9 per cent in 1976 and 8 per cent in 2000) are not significantly different.

Reasons for the phenomenon

There is a very good reason for this outperformance: the UK market also has a tendency to experience sharp falls in the first two years of the cycle.

In fact, the second year of the US presidential cycle marked the end of UK bear markets in five years: 1966, 1970, 1974, 1990 and 1998. There were also significant falls in the UK equity market in 1994 and 2002. In other words, by investing in the UK stock market at the start of the third year of the US election cycle, we can significantly reduce the odds of encountering a down year because there is a high chance that share prices will have already bottomed out well before then.

trading strategy 16

Buy a FTSE All-Share Index tracker in third year of US presidential cycle

With a 100 per cent track record over four decades, and an average annual return of over 28 per cent, it pays to buy a FTSE All-Share Index tracker at the start of the third year of the US presidential cycle. It also pays to keep the position open through the fourth year of the cycle to try and benefit from that hefty 14 per cent average return posted by the UK market in US election years since 1968.

If you want to benefit from this trend, one way to do so is to buy an ETF. ETFs listed on the London Stock Exchange that track the performance of the FTSE All-Share Index include those issued by Lyxor (TIDM: LFAS) and Deutsche Bank (TIDM: XASX).

Alternatively, buying an ETF that tracks the performance of the FTSE 100 is another way of benefiting from this price trend. This is because the FTSE 100 accounts for a hefty 75 per cent weighting in the FTSE All-Share Index, so the two indices move in step. ETFs listed on the London Stock Exchange that track the FTSE 100 include those issued by Lyxor (TIDM: L100), a subsidiary of French investment bank Société Générale, Deutsche Bank (TIDM: XUKX) and Barclays iShares (TIDM: ISF).

8

Summertime blues

The 'livin may have been easy' in George Gershwin's classic song 'Summertime' from his musical *Porgy & Bess*, but it pays for investors to not get too complacent during the summer months.

Over the past two decades, July has been a poor performer, averaging a monthly return of just 0.3 per cent. Fortunately, there is some respite in August, which has rewarded investors with a 1.3 per cent return for the past 20 years. However, it pays to take note when prices fail to keep up with these historic trends.

❝ when shares prices in July take a big hit a bear market is most likely running, if this weakness continues into the first fortnight of August, it's best to reach for your tin hats ❞

Research by stock market historian David Schwartz (2007a) reveals that, in the past 80 years, there have only been 9 occasions when the UK market suffered significant losses in the last three trading weeks of July. True, we can expect some weakness in the penultimate week of the month, as this is one of the worst-performing weeks of the year. This, though, could reflect investor nervousness ahead of the imminent corporate reporting season as FTSE 100 companies with December and June year ends start releasing results in the final week of July. As a result the last week of July is traditionally one of the strongest weeks of the year and this positive momentum at the end of the month seems to carry through into August, one of the best performing months of the year, as has been the case in recent times.

However, when share prices in July take a big hit, then it's worth paying attention as our history books tells us that a bear market is most likely running. In fact, the bears were wreaking havoc on all bar one of those nine occasions.

Moreover, if this market weakness continues into the first fortnight of August, it's best to reach for your tin hats because the statistics point to further market weakness: a bear market was running in 90 per cent of all cases when this has happened (Schwartz, 2007a). Also, if at the end of August share prices have been down during the course of the month, having suffered declines in both June and July, then your portfolio should be placed on red alert.

Mr Schwartz notes that consecutive falls in the three summer months have only happened nine times in the past eight decades and, on every single occasion, share prices have taken a nasty fall (Schwartz, 2008b).

For example, in the early 1990s, equity investors were spooked by movements in the foreign exchange markets, which led to sterling being unceremoniously ejected from the European exchange rate mechanism. This netted legendary hedge fund manager George Soros around $1billion of profits when he gambled successfully that the UK government would be forced to withdraw the pound from the currency fix. Thankfully, investors regained their composure when the penny dropped that a devalued currency was actually *good* news for an economy emerging from a recession.

> **"** falls in the three summer months have only happened nine times in the past eighty decades and, on every single occassion, share prices have taken a nasty fall **"**

Fast forward 15 years to the summer of 2007 and the FTSE All-Share Index fell by over 5 per cent from its all-time high over the summer months, racking up losses in June, July and August. In retrospect, this was the point at which the four-year-old bull market (which started in March 2003) came to a shuddering halt. Between the end of August 2007 and October 2008, the UK stock market went on to fall a further 40 per cent.

Summertime market volatility

At the end of bull markets, volatility in share prices has a habit of rising. That is because the easy gains have already been made. The inflated share price valuations lead to a tussle between optimistic investors looking for even higher share price highs and bearish investors looking for the markets to peak and start a downtrend.

trading strategy 17

Sell if summer share prices weak

Summer may not be a great time to be invested in the market, but it needn't be a terrible time either. If share prices are taking a tumble during June, July and August, however, or have experienced significant weakness in the latter half of July and the first half of August, then the stock market is sending a very strong message that something is wrong.

The strategy is simple: sustained share price weakness over the summer months is a strong bear market signal, so sell your holdings before those summertime blues become an autumn nightmare.

" sustained share price weakness over the summer months is a strong bear market signal "

It pays to take note when market volatility spikes as four decades of stock market history tells us that the bears always end up mauling the bulls when these tussles are over. This is even more important if the sharp rise in market volatility has followed or accompanied share price weakness in the summer as it is a clear warning sign to investors that the bull market is over.

" it pays to take note when market volatility spikes as ... the bears always end up mauling the bulls when these tussles are over "

This was certainly the case after the UK stock market peaked in the summer of 2007. In fact, between the autumn of that year and October 2008, the blue-chip FTSE 100 Index experienced intra-day price moves (taken from the high during the day to the low price) of at least 1 per cent or over during 90 per cent of all trading days in that 12-month period. This is pretty unprecedented, as Mr Schwartz notes, as there have only been 8 other occasions in the past 4 decades when the UK stock market has moved up or down intra-day by at least 1 per cent in more than 50 per cent of all trading days in any 2-month period (Schwartz, 2007b).

In every single one of these cases, the stock market fell by at least 15 per cent from its peak before bottoming out. In most cases, the share price falls were far deeper: ranging from a peak-to-trough decline of 21 per cent in 1981, to a stomach-churning 72 per cent plunge in the 1972–1974 bear market (see Figure 8.1).

The website **www.euroinvestor.co.uk** is very useful for monitoring market volatility and, specifically the opening, closing and daily high

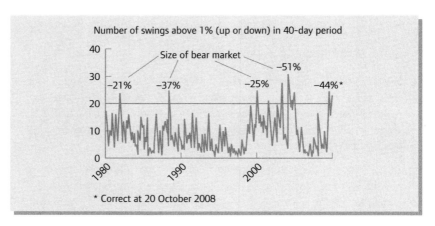

figure 8.1 Extreme volatility points to extreme share price falls

Source: Schwartz, 2007b

and low prices of the FTSE 100 Index. The site is free and price data is available going back ten years, so it is easy to see if the Index is showing unusual levels of market volatility.

trading strategy 18

Heed the warning of summer lows and high volatility

Ignoring significant share price weakness during the summer has been a dangerous trading strategy in the past. However, if this weakness is then followed by a sharp rise in market volatility, it is the final warning signal that the good times are well and truly over and to bank profits if you have not already done so.

Remember, extreme levels of sustained market volatility have led to peak-to-trough declines in the UK stock market of at least 15 per cent in the past four decades. Once extreme market volatility is confirmed, therefore (we are looking for intra-day moves of at least 1 per cent in the FTSE 100 Index for at least half the trading days in a 2-month trading period), we can then use this important bear market signal to make a profit by shorting the market.

The best way to execute a short trade on the FTSE 100 is through a spread bet. The Index is a proxy for the whole UK equity market as it accounts for over 75 per cent of the weighting in the FTSE All-Share Index. In the UK, the leading spread betting firms are IG Index, City Index, Cantor Index, CMC Markets and Capital Spreads. The benefits of carrying out this trade this way are two-fold. First, profits are tax free under the current tax regime in the UK. Second, profits are easy to calculate as you can bet the FTSE 100 will fall from as little as £1 a point movement in the Index with some firms.

chapter

9

Predictive powers

magine having a system that is able to predict, with uncanny accuracy, how stock markets will perform over the course of the year. Incredibly, academics Michael Cooper, John McConnell and Alexai Ovtchinnikov have done just that.

January's predictive powers

In their paper, 'The other January effect' (2006), they detail their analysis of the performance of the US equity market for the period 1940–2003. Their aim was to find out whether or not there was a relationship between how the market performed in January and its subsequent performance over the rest of the year. The results of the study were quite a revelation.

Cooper, McConnell and Ovtchinnikov found that, when the S&P 500 Index rose in the month of January, on average it then went on to produce a very healthy 14.8 per cent return over the next 11 months of the year. However, when the market fell in January, it was a different story altogether, with the return over the remainder of the year being a disappointing 2.9 per cent on average. That's no better than investors earn by holding risk-free government bonds.

ff using the positive return from January as a predictor boasts an incredible 88 per cent strike rate since 1940 ff

In the study, the academics noted that, of the 41 months when share prices rose in January, there were only 5 occasions when the return from the following 11 months was negative. In other words, using the positive return from January as a predictor of how share prices will perform over the remainder of the year boasted an incredible 88 per cent strike rate since 1940. It's worth noting that, of the five years when the January buy signal failed, it then took some extraordinary events to derail the market from returning positive gains in the following 11 months. For example, in 1966 investors had to contend with the Vietnam War, while in 2001 stock markets were rocked by the events of 9/11.

By contrast, the study found that shares are more likely to fall than rise over the subsequent 11 months if they have fallen in January. In fact, in the remainder of the year, share prices went on to fall in 14 of the 23 years when January produced a negative return.

> 66 January's amazing predictive powers have shown no sign of waning in recent years, in 2004, 2006 and 2007, the S&P 500 rose in the month and went on to rise by 6.7 per cent, 10.7 per cent and 2 per cent, respectively, in the remainder of the year 99

Moreover, January's amazing predictive powers have shown no sign of waning in recent years. In 2004, 2006 and 2007, the S&P 500 rose during the month and then went on to rise by 6.7 per cent, 10.7 per cent and 2 per cent, respectively, in the remainder of the year. However, when the Index dropped in January 2005, this correctly signalled a poor year ahead, with the Index only managing to rise a miserly 3 per cent over the course of the whole year. The signal flashed again in January 2008 when the S&P Index fell 6.1 per cent in the month. By mid-October the Index had fallen a further 40 per cent.

Interestingly, the academics found that the effect persists:

"after controlling for macroeconomic/business cycle variables that have been shown to predict stock returns, the presidential cycle in returns, and investor sentiment. The January effect also persists among both large and small capitalization stocks and among both value and glamour stocks."

Reasons for the phenomenon

It should not come as a major surprise that share prices have risen 65 per cent of the time during January since 1940. January is also the third best month of the year, with the S&P 500 rising by around 1.4 per cent, on average, in the past seven decades. The fact that the S&P 500 *continues* to rise around 88 per cent of the time over the remainder of the year after rising in January is more difficult to explain, however.

Not even the academics have managed to come up with an explanation for that. One factor that helps, though, is the clear bias of investment returns in the course of the US presidential sycle (see Chapter 7). For instance, the third and fourth years of the US presidential cycle have a great record for producing decent returns for investors. Since 1967, there have been only 2 down election years in this 40-year period, with all the other 19 election and pre-election years posting positive gains. This narrows the odds considerably that the market will rise between the start of February and the end of December.

trading strategy 19

Monitor January

The saying that 'As January goes, so goes the rest of the year' not only has the backing of a wealth of academic studies but it also boasts one of the best track records there is: 88 per cent success rate in predicting that the market will rise in the remainder of the year if it rises in January.

We can improve the odds of making a winning trade even further as we know that election and pre-election years are great times to be invested in the market. So if the S&P 500 Index rises in January in either one of these two years, then you should take note and buy an index tracker at the end of the month. The best way to execute this trade is through an ETF listed on the London Stock Exchange that tracks the performance of the S&P 500 Index, such as Barclays iShares (TIDM: IUSA).

It's also worth taking notice if January is a poor month. The statistics are weighted towards a disappointing year ahead, on average, if prices fall during the month. That's reason enough to take a more cautious view on your shareholdings, especially if the January price falls take place during the historically poor-performing first or second years of the US presidential cycle.

The January effect on the UK stock market

❝ the UK does show a decided January effect under certain conditions when prices in January fall sharply, this is a great predictor for future returns ❞

The question for most investors is that, if there is a January effect with predictive powers operating in the US stock market, then is this an international phenomenon? Academics Martin Bohl and Christian Salm (2007) looked into this, extending Cooper, McConnell and Ovtchinnikov's (2006) study to incorporate stock market trends across 14 countries. They found that, although the predictive effect was clearly working in the US, only two other countries – Holland and Norway – exhibited a similar peculiarity. They dismissed the UK market as having no January predictive effect at all. However, I have found that the UK most definitely does show a decided January effect under certain conditions.

True, the UK stock market has historically only risen 72 per cent of the time between February and December following a January advance – 16 percentage points less than in the US. Moreover the market rises two thirds of the time in these 11 months anyway, irrespective of what happens in January. So, on the face of it, Bohl and Salm appear correct that January advances have no predictive powers regarding determining returns for the rest of the year. However, it would be a mistake to make that assumption because we can tilt the odds heavily in our favour by analysing the degree of the price movements in January and subsequent returns.

❝ there are only 11 occasions when the UK stock market has fallen more than 3.12 per cent in January ... in only 2 years did the UK stock market rise between February and December ❞

Research by stock market historian David Schwartz (2006a) notes that when prices in January fall sharply, this is a great predictor for future returns. In the past 90 years, there are only 11 occasions when the UK stock market has fallen more than 3.12 per cent in January. In 7 of those 11 years, it then fell in the subsequent 11 months and, in another 2 years, it was virtually flat for the remainder of the year.

So, in only 2 of those 11 years did the UK stock market manage to rise between February and December after taking a big hit in January. In other words, there has only been a 1 in 5 chance of the market rising under these conditions for the past 90 years.

This trend has great relevance as the UK stock market fell heavily in January 2008, with the FTSE 100 Index falling from 6480 at the start of the month to 5880 at the end of the month – a thumping loss of 9 per cent over the month. That made it number 12 in the series. True to form, the market fell heavily in 2008, dropping a further 35 per cent by mid-October.

Reasons for the phenomenon

Big share price hits in January are a worry because the winter months are seasonally the best time to be invested in the market (see Chapter 5).

❝ big share price hits in January are a worry because the winter months are seasonally the best time to be invested ❞

So, if the market is struggling when it has a seasonal headwind, investors have to ask if the market is sending out an early warning signal that all is not well, as was clearly the case in January 2008. This hardly augurs well for its performance over the weaker six-month May to October period, which has historically produced meagre returns for investors.

trading strategy 20

Short sell if the prices fall in January

Short selling the market at the end of January looks like an attractive trade if it has suffered a heavy hit during the month. Remember, 90 years of stock market history tell us that there has only been a 1 in 5 chance that it will rise over the next 11 months and a near 80 per cent chance that it will fall or end the year flat at best. Also, from those years we have learned that there is a high probability that share prices will be lower at some point in the 11-month period between February and December, offering alert investors the opportunity to bank profits if the market has fallen significantly.

The most flexible option for shorting the UK market is through spread betting on the FTSE 100, whereby investors place a down bet on every point movement in the Index with a spread betting firm. Profits from spread betting are currently tax free in the UK. Alternatively, most stockbrokers offer contracts for difference (another form of leverage trading), whereby investors can either buy or sell the underlying index and profit from movements in that index.

❝ short selling the market at the end of January looks like an attractive trade if it has suffered a heavy hit during the month ❞

The January to May stock market effect

Share price rises in January may not have much statistical significance for predicting the direction of the UK stock market for the rest of the year, but there is one great buying signal that has worked fantastically well: the January to May effect. There is a very good reason for it, too.

Using price data for the past 40 years, stock market historian David Schwartz notes that there were 21 years when the UK stock market rose in this 5-month period by up to 15.5 per cent. Amazingly, share prices then went on to rise over the remainder of the year in all bar two of those years.

Even the exceptions to the rule hardly dented investors' portfolios. In 1981, the market recovered from a heavy hit in the late summer to end down a meagre 0.78 per cent in the 7-month period of June to December.

It was a similar story in 2007 when the UK market, which was 6.4 per cent ahead after the first 5 months of the year, took a tumble in the summer, but managed to recover most of the losses to end the 7-month period down only 2.1 per cent.

Reasons for the phenomenon

The winter and early spring months are a great time to be invested in the market. In the three-month period between the start of January and the end of March, the FTSE All-Share Index has risen by an average of 4.4 per cent since 1980, posting only 6 down years in that 27-year period. April is also a good time to be holding equities as it is one of the strongest per-forming months of in the year. Combine these historic seasonal trends (see Chapter 5) and you can see why share prices have a great chance of rising in the first four months of the year.

sharp hits in May and the first half of June are seriously bad news as it is a near certainty that a bear market is in progress

May, however, is a treacherous month (see Chapter 19), with investors regularly taking a hefty hit to their portfolios every five or six years or so. When this happens, the losses in May can easily wipe out the gains made during the previous four months. Moreover, sharp hits in May and the first half of June are seriously bad news as it is a near certainty that a bear market is in progress. In fact, in the past 72 years, there have been only 11 occasions when share prices have fallen by at least 7 per cent in the 30 trading days from the start of May (Schwartz, 2006c).

in the past 72 years, there have been only 11 occasions when share prices have fallen by at least 7 per cent in the 30 trading days from the start of May

Worryingly, a bear market was running in all bar one of these periods.

So, if the UK market can avoid a poor May and ends the month in the black, the odds of a bear market being in progress are much reduced. Clearly, this augurs well for the market's performance for the remainder of the year as the bull market will still be running. Equally, if the winter and spring seasonal trends are working well, then this is another positive associated with bull market years.

Buy a FTSE 100 Index tracker end May

Buying a FTSE 100 Index tracker at the end of May and running the position until the end of the year has proved a pretty low-risk trading strategy for the past four decades. The trade has proved profitable in 19 of the 21 years when the market has posted a positive return of up to 15.5 per cent in the first 5 months of the year. Even when this trade has failed to turn a profit by the year end, the downside has hardly been a painful experience: a loss of 0.78 per cent in 1981 and 2.1 per cent in 2007.

One way to execute this trade is to use unleveraged products, such as ETFs, that track the performance of the FTSE 100, with each 1 per cent movement in the Index translating to a 1 per cent movement in the ETF. These include those issued by Lyxor (TIDM: L100), a subsidiary of French investment bank Société Générale, Deutsche Bank (TIDM: XUKX) and Barclays iShares (TIDM: ISF). ETFs can be bought or sold through stockbrokers in the same way as shares in any listed company.

10

Santa Claus rally

C hristmas is always an expensive time of the year, but not for everyone. That's because the really smart money will have already
racked up gains playing the markets during the final month of the
year. It's not a lottery either because December is one of the most profitable months to be invested in equities.

Santa Claus delivers early

In fact, since 1980, the FTSE All-Share Index has risen no fewer than 22
times during the month and only fallen 6 times. That's a success rate of
75 per cent. Moreover, the average monthly gain is a very healthy 1.99
per cent, even after accounting for those 6 down months. Taking a closer
look at the statistics (see Table 10.1), it is apparent
that it takes something pretty significant to derail
the UK market during December.

> **the really smart
> money will have
> already racked up
> gains playing the
> markets during the
> final month of the
> year, it takes
> something pretty
> significant to derail
> the UK market during
> December**

In 1980, it was political strife during Margaret
Thatcher's first term in office and a UK recession
that sent the market tumbling by almost 5 per
cent. Fast forward 22 years and the 2000–2003
bear market got its claws into investors' portfolios
in 2002, sending stocks down by a similar
amount. However, these kinds of losses are pretty
rare and it's worth noting that the other four
down December months in the past three decades
were not major losers.

table 10.1 Performance of FTSE All-Share Index in December since 1980

Year	UK market monthly return (%)
1980	−4.89
1981	−0.64
1982	1.81
1983	1.87
1984	5.83
1985	−1.95
1986	2.47
1987	9.28
1988	−0.73
1989	5.80
1990	0.01
1991	1.60
1992	3.87
1993	8.08
1994	−0.44
1995	0.81
1996	1.44
1997	5.35
1998	1.79
1999	5.03
2000	1.32
2001	0.39
2002	−5.45
2003	2.83
2004	2.79
2005	3.87
2006	3.26
2007	0.18
Monthly return	1.99
Up years	22
Down years	6

Source: Thomson Reuters Datastream

What's more, when the market rises during December, it posts big gains, with the average increase in the FTSE All-Share Index during the month being an eye-watering 3.17 per cent during those 22 up years. That more than compensates for the risk of a bad down month, of which we really only have had two in the past three decades.

Reasons for the phenomenon

There are a variety of reasons for the market being more likely to rise than fall during the month of December. For starters, the period marks the end of the year and there could be some window dressing by fund managers and market participants chasing end-of-year bonuses. Also, history tells us that the six-month period from the end of October to the end of April is the best time to be invested in equities and, in particular, the fourth quarter of the year. In fact, the UK stock market has only fallen six times in the final quarter of the year since 1980. Even allowing for those down quarters, that three-month period has still managed to post an average quarterly gain of 4.3 per cent in the 28-year period. This is reassuring for investors who decide to put their chips on the table during this seasonally strong period for investing.

❝ the UK stock market has only fallen six times in the final quarter of the year since 1980 ❞

The smart money also knows that the chance of taking a big hit during December is far less than at other times of the year. For instance, even during bear markets, the size of decline (around 0.5 per cent on average) seen during the month has been relatively modest. It's worth noting, too, that, in the past four decades, the UK stock market has only been in a bear market four times during the month of December. So the chances of making a loss are not only much reduced but also any potential hit is unlikely to be severe during the month. In turn, investors may be less risk averse in December and more likely to play the markets.

There is another very important reason for December being such a consistent money spinner: the month is split in two, with the odds of the market rising in the second half of the month not only significantly better than the first but also the total return generated during December is skewed to the second half of the month. This has everything to do with Christmas falling in the final week of the month, which has a direct effect on how markets behave around that time of the year.

It is a common to see trading volumes tail off in the run-up to Christmas as dealers and City professionals shut up shop for the festive period. As a result of this, liquidity starts to dry up and, given that the only market participants still trading are likely to be buyers of stocks, then, in the absence of sellers, we have conditions ripe for the market to rise on very low volumes. That is exactly what happens.

Improving the odds of a happy Christmas

In the past 26 years, the UK market has risen no fewer than 22 times in the period 11 December to 5 January, only falling 4 times. This is an amazing run, with a success rate of showing a profit almost 85 per cent of the time.

❝ in the past 26 years, the UK market has risen no fewer than 22 times in the period 11 December to 5 January, only falling 4 times ❞

What's more, the average gain is 2.47 per cent over this 25-day period. That thumping profit is not only greater than the 2 per cent average return posted for the whole of the month of December but also there are fewer down days, so the risk of banking a loss on this trade is lower, too. By comparison, the odds of the UK market rising in the first 10 days of the month are roughly 50:50.

trading strategy 22

Buy a FTSE All-Share Index tracker 11 December

It may be tempting to buy a FTSE All-Share Index tracker at the end of November and just sit back and rake in the gains. However, the smart money will wait until 11 December before making a move. The strategy is to hold this position open until 5 January to benefit from accentuated moves over the Christmas trading period when buyers have far greater influence over market prices than normal, due to reduced liquidity and lighter trading volumes. Remember, this 25-day trade has returned 2.47 per cent, on average, for the past 28 years, with an 85 per cent success rate.

ETFs listed on the London Stock Exchange that track the performance of the FTSE All-Share Index include those issued by Lyxor (TIDM: LFAS), a subsidiary of French investment bank Société Générale and Deutsche Bank (TIDM: XASX).

An alternative way to track the UK market is to buy an ETF that tracks the performance of the FTSE 100, which accounts for a weighting of around 75 per cent in the FTSE All-Share Index. ETFs listed on the London Stock Exchange include those issued by Lyxor (TIDM: L100), a subsidiary of French investment bank Société Générale, Deutsche Bank

(TIDM: XUKX) and Barclays iShares (TIDM: ISF). ETFs can be bought or sold through stockbrokers in the same way as shares in any listed company.

The final way to execute this trade is through an up spread bet on the FTSE 100 through a spread betting firm. In the UK, these include companies such as City Index, IG Index, Capital Spreads, CMC Markets and Cantor Index. Profits from spread betting are currently tax free in the UK and you can place a bet from as little as £1 per point on movements in the Index.

trading strategy 23

Last-minute Christmas shopping

There is a second way to play the Christmas markets. It may not be a well-known fact, but, for the reasons mentioned above – low liquidity and trading volumes, lack of sellers and most trades are buys – it is pretty unusual to lose money by investing in the stock market on Christmas Eve and running this position through to the first trading day of January. This is because Christmas Eve – 27 and 28 December, which have relatively light trading in the UK – are some of the strongest trading days of the year.

In fact, the UK market has, on average, risen over 75 per cent of the time in the 2 trading days prior to Christmas and the 3 trading days following Boxing Day. Given that the week beginning 29 December just happens to historically be one of the best trading weeks of the year, you can see why this trade has proved a winner over the years.

So, the second option for a Christmas trade is to open an up spread bet on the FTSE 100 or buy a FTSE 100 Index tracking ETF during the week before Christmas and, specifically, two days before 25 December. The strategy is to run this position until the first trading day of the New Year. This period has some of the strongest trading days of the year, which, again, is hardly surprising given that volumes are light and buyers have undue influence over market movements.

"the UK market has risen over 75 per cent of the time in the 2 trading days prior to Christmas and the 3 trading days following Boxing Day"

US market returns in December

Not surprisingly, a similar December effect occurs in the US, with the Dow Jones Industrial Average rising around two thirds of the time during the month of December. However, the effect is far less strong than in the UK, with the average monthly return being 1.59 per cent on the Dow (see Table

10.2) compared with almost 2 per cent on the FTSE All-Share Index. Moreover, with nine down months since 1980, the chances of booking a loss during December is far greater in the US than in the UK.

table 10.2 Performance of Dow Jones Industrial Average Index in December since 1980

Year	US market monthly return (%)
1980	−2.95
1981	−1.57
1982	0.70
1983	−1.36
1984	1.90
1985	5.06
1986	−0.95
1987	5.74
1988	2.56
1989	1.73
1990	2.89
1991	9.47
1992	−0.12
1993	1.90
1994	2.55
1995	0.84
1996	−1.13
1997	1.09
1998	0.71
1999	5.69
2000	3.58
2001	1.72
2002	−6.23
2003	6.86
2004	3.40
2005	−0.82
2006	1.97
2007	−0.79
Monthly return	**1.59**
Up years	19
Down years	9

Source: Thomson Reuters Datastream

> **a similar December effect occurs in the US, with the Dow Jones Industrial Average rising around two thirds of the time during the month of December**

Don't think that this means that a pair trade would work either. As we have seen, this trade is when you buy an index tracker or place an up spread bet on the stronger market (FTSE 100 or FTSE All-Share) and simultaneously short sell through a down spread bet the weaker market (Dow Jones Industrial Average). The aim is to try to profit from the tendency of one of the markets to outperform the other. In fact, this would have been a terrible trade, losing money in 13 of the past 28 years. The reason for this is that, when the US and UK stock markets rise in December, the average return on both indices is identical at 3.17 per cent, but, during down months, the losses on the FTSE All-Share are deeper.

> **when the US and UK stock markets rise in December, the average return on both indices is identical at 3.17 per cent, but, during down months, the losses on the FTSE All-Share are deeper**

So, given that a pair trade is far too risky and the return from the US market is below that from the UK market during the month December, with more down months in any case, then the preferred option is the low-risk trade on the FTSE All-Share or FTSE 100 outlined in trading strategy 22. This has proved the most profitable investment strategy and also boasts a better risk:reward than playing the Dow Jones Industrial Average.

trading strategy 24

Christmas shopping in the Big Apple

It's no coincidence that the UK trading strategy of going long of the UK market a couple of days before Christmas and keeping the position open into the first week of January also seems to work for US markets. When market volumes and liquidity are lower than normal and the sellers are more interested in Christmas festivities than playing the markets, then Wall Street's buyers also have a greater influence than normal.

The facts seem to back this up. Over this two-week trading period, the broader-based S&P 500 Index has generated a positive return of around 1.37 per cent and boasts a success rate of around 75 per cent, making this a strategy worth trading.

ETFs listed on the London Stock Exchange that track the performance of the S&P 500 Index include, Barclays iShares (TIDM: IUSA). Alternatively, you can place a spread up bet on this Index through a spread betting firm. It's worth noting that, although the S&P 500 is denominated in dollars, a spread bet can be placed in sterling for every point movement in the Index. Any profit or gain made would also be in sterling, so this method of executing the trade avoids the risk of exchange rates moving against you.

One note of caution. If Santa decides to stay at home and the seasonal year end December rally fails to materialise, this is a leading indicator of future market weakness. One bad Christmas is par for the course, but ignoring this warning sign could mean you may lose much more than a few presents.

❝ if Santa decides to stay at home and the seasonal year end December rally fails to materialise, this is a leading indicator of future market weakness ❞

In fact, a big hit over this two-week trading period is a red alert for the markets. That is exactly what happened in 2007 when the trade actually showed a loss of 3.4 per cent and the S&P 500 fell by 0.9 per cent in December. The Index consequently fell 40 per cent between the first week of January 2008 and mid-October 2008. That wasn't a one-off either, as the 4 per cent loss on the trade in 1999 was the precursor to the savage 2000–2002 US bear market.

chapter

Religious holidays

I n previous chapters, I have shown how changes in our mood can impact behaviour patterns and how this can affect our investment decisions (see Chapters 3 and 5). In the same way, it is not surprising that religious festivals impact our behaviour, too.

> **❝ changes in our mood can impact behaviour patterns and affect our investment decisions ❞**

Jewish holy days

In the study 'Testing for non-secular regularities in stock returns and trading activity', academics Laura Frieder and Avanidhar Subrahmanyam (2003) looked into how the US stock market performed around the most sacred of Jewish holidays, Rosh Hashanah and Yom Kippur. The former is an uplifting occasion, signifying the Jewish New Year and God's creation of the world. At this time, many Jews spend the day in prayer, hoping to be granted a good year. By contrast Yom Kippur, the Day of Attonement, falls nine days later and is an austere occasion. It is a solemn day of fasting and regret for past misdeeds. Many Jews will spend the day in prayer, asking God for forgiveness to begin the New Year with a clean slate.

> **❝ the S&P 500 Index rose by 1.14 per cent, on average, on the days around Rosh Hashanah ❞**

Analysing price data for the S&P 500 for the period 1946 to 2000, Frieder and Subrahmanyam found that, two days before Rosh Hashanah, the Index rose by an average of 0.35 per cent, by 0.28 per cent the day before, 0.23 per cent on the day itself and 0.28 per cent on the day after the religious holiday. That's 1.14 per cent, on average, on the days around Rosh Hashanah. By contrast, in the two days leading up to Yom Kippur, the Index rose by a meagre 0.15 per cent, on average – less than two points on the S&P 500 Index. On the day of Yom Kippur itself, the Index then fell, on average, by 0.18 per cent and by the same amount the following day. In other words, despite the festivals being only nine days apart and falling in the months of September and October each year, there is a marked difference in the investment returns around these Jewish holy days (see Table 11.1).

> despite being only nine days apart there is a marked difference in the investment returns around these Jewish holy days

table 11.1 Returns on S&P 500 around Holy Jewish Festivals of Rosh Hashanah and Yom Kippur (1943–2000)

Religious Festival		Percentage average daily change in S&P 500 Index (%)				
		Two days before	One day before	On the day	Day after	Two days after
Rosh Hashanah	Mean	0.35	0.28	0.23	0.28	0.14
	Median	0.26	0.26	0.25	0.04	0.12
Yom Kippur	Mean	0.01	0.14	−0.18	−0.18	−0.10
	Median	−0.08	0.00	0.01	−0.07	−0.05

Source: The Anderson School of Management, University of California

Reasons for the phenomenon

Rosh Hashanah is an uplifting experience and this is reflected in the trading activity of Jews in the days surrounding this festival. It would be logical for the positive mood of this group of investors to lead to greater investor confidence, so boosting their appetite to take on greater risk. In turn, this appears to feed through to buying activity and a run-up in stock prices.

> Rosh Hashanah is an uplifting experience and this is reflected in the trading activity of Jews in the days surrounding this holy day

By contrast, Yom Kippur is a solemn occasion, which is likely to have a negative impact on the mood of this group of investors. This feeds through in higher risk aversion and less confidence in the market. Hence, the fall in stock prices, on average, on the day of Yom Kippur and the day following this religious holy day.

" Yom Kippur is a solemn occasion, this feeds through in higher risk aversion and less confidence in the market **""**

" given the substantial wealth and assets this small community control, it is actually quite logical for their influence on the financial markets to be disproportionately large **""**

" the price behaviour ... is mirrored in Israel's stock market, with the ... Index rising by 0.82 per cent on the day after Rosh Hashanah, but falling by 0.5 per cent on the day after Yom Kippur **""**

It may seem odd that these Jewish holy days can have such a dramatic effect on trading on the world's most liquid and largest stock market, given that the Jewish community only accounts for around 2 per cent of the population in the US. However, it's worth remembering that the Jewish population is significant in terms of wealth, with family incomes around 70 per cent higher than the US national average. Moreover, they are a very important force in the financial arena, as can be seen from investment firms such as Goldman Sachs. So, given the substantial wealth and assets this small community control, it is actually quite logical for their influence on the financial markets to be disproportionate to their numbers.

Interestingly, Frieder and Subrahmanyam found that the price behaviour in the US market around these high holy days is mirrored in Israel's stock market, with the Israel Share and Convertible Index rising by 0.82 per cent on the day after Rosh Hashanah, but falling by 0.5 per cent on the day after Yom Kippur.

As there are significant wealthy Jewish communities in countries outside the US and a third of all trades on the US stock market are carried out by overseas investors, then, if some of these investors are affected in a similar way by the Jewish holy days, this will clearly have a direct impact on how the US stock market performs.

trading strategy 25

Rosh Hashanah

The obvious strategy is to buy a S&P 500 Index tracker two days before Rosh Hashanah and close the trade out when the two day festival finishes. In the past, this trade has produced an average return of 1.1 per cent over the 4 trading days and in 2008 returned a profit of around 0.5 per cent. ETFs listed on the London Stock Exchange that track the performance of the S&P 500 Index include Barclays iShares (TIDM: IUSA).

Alternatively, this trade can be executed through an up spread bet on the S&P 500 Index through a spread betting firm. In the UK these include companies such as City Index, IG Index, Capital Spreads, CMC Markets and Cantor Index. Profits from spread betting are currently tax free in the UK and you can place a bet from as little as £1 per point on movements in the Index. Please note, though, that the S&P 500 Index is denominated in dollars, but there is no currency risk as you can place a sterling bet on every point movement in the Index and your trade will be settled in sterling.

Rosh Hashanah in 2009 falls on Friday 18 September, so, to use this strategy, buy the S&P 500 Index tracker at the start of trading on Thursday 17 September and close out the position at close of trading on Tuesday 21 September. The dates for Rosh Hashanah for the following years are: Wednesday 8 September 2010, Wednesday 28 September 2011, Sunday 16 September 2012, Wednesday 4 September 2013, Wednesday 24 September 2014 and Sunday 13 September 2015.

❝ buy a S&P 500 Index tracker two days before Rosh Hashanah and close the trade out the day after this holy day ❞

trading strategy 26

Yom Kippur

It is also tempting to try and make a profit by selling the S&P 500 Index at the start of trading on the day of Yom Kippur and buying it back at the close of the following day. The US market has fallen by 0.35 per cent on average during this two-day period. The easiest way to execute this trade is by placing a down spread bet on the Index through a spread betting firm. In October 2008, this two-day trade returned a profit of 8.6 per cent.

Yom Kippur next starts at sundown on Sunday 27 September 2009 and ends at nightfall on Monday 28 September, so, to use this strategy, sell the S&P 500 on Monday 28 September and close the position at the end of trading on Tuesday 29 September 2009 to profit from the expected fall in the Index. The dates for Yom Kippur for the following years are: Friday 17 September 2010, Friday 7 October 2011, Tuesday 25 September 2012, Friday 13 September 2013, Friday 3 October 2014 and Tuesday 22 September 2015.

> **make a profit by selling the S&P 500 Index at the start of trading on the day of Yom Kippur buying it back the following day**

St Patrick's day

As Jewish religious holidays can impact the US stock market, academics Frieder and Subrahmanyam (2003) looked at the performance of the market between 1946 and 2000 around the time of St Patrick's day. This is traditionally a Catholic holy day and was first celebrated over 300 years ago in honour of Saint Patrick, a successful missionary. Since then, it has become a joyful occasion, with the Irish community celebrating the day, which falls on 17 March each year, by drinking and parading. This enjoyment seems to spill over to buoy up investors, with the US stock market rising, on average, by 0.34 per cent two trading days prior to St Patrick's day, 0.37 per cent the day before, 0.07 per cent on the day itself and 0.19 per cent on the day after. Cumulatively, that is a return of 0.97 per cent for the 4-day period.

> **St Patrick's day enjoyment seems to spill over to buoy up investors, with the US stock market rising 0.97 per cent for the 4-day period**

The trend for prices to rise around St Patrick's day still seems to be working, with the S&P 500 rising by 1.7 per cent from 1308 to 1330 for the 4-day trading period in March 2008. This was even more impressive considering that if took place during a savage bear market! This wasn't a one-off either, with the Index posting a gain of 1.6 per cent during this 4-day trading period in 2007 and 0.6 per cent in 2006.

Reasons for this phenomenon

True, part of these healthy gains could result from the fact that March is a good time of the year to be invested in equities. However, the average return on the four trading days around St Patrick's day accounts for virtually *all* of the 0.97 per cent return the S&P 500 Index has averaged for the month of March in the past 6 decades. That's astonishing, so perhaps there is another factor at play here?

> **another reason for the tendency for the market to rise in this four-day period is its crossover with triple witching week**

Another reason for the tendency for the market to rise in this four-day period is its crossover with triple witching week (TWW), when stock options, index options and index futures all expire. This can give the S&P 500 Index a boost as traders settling these options and index contracts may be forced to buy in the market to close their positions out. At least the market has risen more often than it has fallen during TWW in March for the past two decades. As Triple witching day in the first quarter falls on the third Friday of March, there is more often than not some crossover with St Patrick's day.

trading strategy 27

St Patrick's day

The standout trading strategy is to buy a S&P 500 Index tracker two days before St Patrick's day and look to take profits at the close of trading the day after the festival to try and capture the near 1 per cent average rise in the Index for this 4-day trading period. ETFs listed on the London Stock Exchange that track the performance of the S&P 500 Index include Barclays iShares (TIDM: IUSA). Alternatively, the Index can be bought through a spread bet.

St Patrick's day falls on Tuesday 17 March 2009, so the strategy is to buy the index tracker on Friday 13 March 2009 and close the position out on Wednesday 18 March. In subsequent years, St Patrick's day falls on Wednesday 17 March 2010, Thursday 17 March 2011 and Saturday 17 March 2012.

❝ the standout trading strategy is to buy a S&P 500 Index tracker two days before St Patrick's day ❞

12

Extreme market movements

The great advantage of studying the history of the stock market – and specific price trends in particular – is that we can quickly identify certain patterns forming that bear a scary resemblance to ones from the past. History may not repeat itself in exactly the same way, but, in some cases, it gets eerily close. That's why the words 'It's different this time' are probably the most misused words in financial circles. It is very rarely different. In fact, when these words are used by financial experts – as was the case at the top of the dot.com boom and the credit cycle in 2007 to justify heady sky high valuations and rock bottom yields on financial assets – then this is a warning signal that a market top is not far away.

> " "it's different this time" are probably the most misused words in financial circles "

> " the bull market that had started in March 2003 had been rising in an upward channel for a lengthy 53 months by August 2007 "

Channel trading

In 2007, I spent a considerable amount of time analysing bull market channels that have occurred in the UK stock market (Thompson, 2007d, 2007e). This had great relevance at the time as the bull market that had started in March 2003 had been rising in an upward channel for a lengthy 53 months by August 2007 (see Figure 12.1). The lower rising trend line acted as a support for the FTSE 100 Index, with the market bouncing off this trend line, while the upside was being capped by the upper rising trend line (see Figure 12.1).

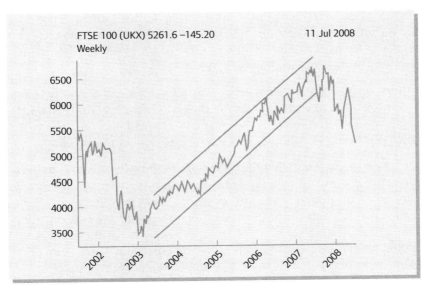

figure 12.1 FTSE 100 bull market trading channel (2003–2007)

Source: Stockcube Research, 2008

Clearly at some point the FTSE 100 would have to break out of this channel. It did so in August 2007 – the Index breached the down side of the channel, which was positioned at 6270. As can be seen from the subsequent price performance, the breach of the channel had great significance because, within one year (by mid-July 2008), the FTSE 100 was trading 1200 points lower, at 5070 – a drop of almost 20 per cent. In other words, the breach of the channel to the down side was an early warning to investors that not only was the 2003–2007 bull market over but also prices were heading significantly lower for the medium-term.

> **❝ the breach of the channel to the down side was an early warning that not only was the bull market over but also prices were heading significantly lower for the medium-term ❞**

Fortunately, I had been alerted to this possibility a year earlier by some research by stock market historian David Schwartz (2006d). Mr Schwartz noted that, in the past 4 decades, there have been 14 other trading channels in the UK market like the one that took place between 2003 and 2007. Of those channels, which all lasted a minimum of 12 months, all bar 1 ended within 24 months of starting. The exception was the bull market that ran between 1994 and 1997, which held prices in a rising channel for 35 months.

Therefore, the 2003–2007 bull market was by far the longest period that the UK market had been contained within a rising trading channel, so a break-out was well overdue by the summer of 2007. The important question was, 'Which way will prices break?'

History, again, is instrumental here, as Mr Schwartz found that prices broke to the down side in all but a couple of these 15 bull market rising channels. Moreover, once the bottom of the channel was penetrated, the break to the down side from this point was generally a minimum of 10 per cent.

Mr Schwartz also found that the exceptions to the rule (when prices broke the upper rising trend line) did not have a happy ending. For instance, in 1986, the bull market went into overdrive, penetrating the top of the rising channel, and continued rising for another 14 months until July 1987. The stock market crash of October 1987 was hardly the fairy tale ending investors buying into this rally were envisaging, with share prices plunging by over a third between July and November of that year.

It was a similar story a decade later, in 1997, with the FTSE 100 pushing through the top of the rising channel and peaking out in late July 1998. The Russian bond crisis that year and the collapse of hedge fund Long-Term Capital Management sent share prices crashing, with the FTSE 100 plunging over 25 per cent, from 6183 to 4600, between 21 July and early October 1998.

> ❝ when bull markets eventually top out ... share prices retrace a significant amount of the gains made, it is therefore hardly surprising that bull market channels have a habit of breaking to the down side ❞

Reasons for the phenomenon

When a rising channel forms and share prices move between the lower and upper trend lines for a prolonged period – as was the case in 2003–2007 – then it is associated with bull markets. These are periods when the stock market moves up by at least 15 to 20 per cent from the trough of the previous bear market. However, we know from previous chapters that when bull markets eventually top out (Chapter 1), this is always followed by a period when share prices retrace a significant amount of the gains made during that bull run (Chapter 2). It is therefore hardly surprising that bull market channels like these have a habit of breaking to the down side as, the longer they run, the greater are the gains that are made and the shorter the odds that the final move will be a break of the *lower* channel.

> ❝ once a bull market trading channel has formed, the odds of the Index breaking out to the up side are pretty long ❞

Profit from trading the channel

Once a bull market trading channel has been formed, the odds of the Index
penetrating the upper rising trend line and breaking out to the up side are pretty
long. We can use this to our advantage by taking a move of the Index to the upper
trend line as a signal to take profits on our shareholdings, with the intention of
buying them back once the market bounces off the lower rising trend line. If you
had used this simple trading strategy during the 2003–2007 bull market, when
the FTSE 100 Index rose by 105 per cent from trough-to-peak, you would have
made significant gains well in excess of this figure. That is because this trading
strategy maximises profits from the up moves, but avoids giving these gains back
when the market retraces its steps back to the lower rising price channel.

One way to trade the Index in this way is through an ETF that tracks the
performance of the FTSE 100 Index. ETFs listed on the London Stock Exchange
include those issued by Lyxor (TIDM: L100), a subsidiary of French investment
bank Société Générale, Deutsche Bank (TIDM: XUKX) and Barclays iShares (TIDM:
ISF). ETFs are traded in the same way as ordinary shares and have the additional
benefit of being exempt from UK stamp duty when purchased.

Remember, though, that the longer the FTSE 100 moves in an upwards trading
channel, the more likely the Index is to break out of the channel as all bar a
couple of the 15 channels from the past 4 decades ended within 2 years. It is
therefore best to buy back the ETF once the Index has successfully bounced off
the bottom of the channel to mitigate the risk of it penetrating through the lower
rising trend line.

Sell when the Index breaks the lower trend line

If the FTSE 100 fails to bounce off the lower rising channel and breaks to the
down side, that is very bearish. History tells us that the odds are heavily weighted
towards there being a significant drop in share prices once the bottom of the
channel has been penetrated.

In the past, short selling the FTSE 100 once it has broken through the lower rising
trend line of the channel has proved a profitable trade as prices generally fall
another 10 per cent from this point at the very least. The easiest way to execute
this trade is by placing a spread bet to sell the Index through a spread betting
firm. In the UK, these include companies such as City Index, IG Index, Capital

▶

Spreads, CMC Markets and Cantor Index. Profits from spread betting are currently tax free in the UK and you can place a bet on every point movement in the Index from as little as £1 per point.

" if the FTSE 100 fails to bounce off the lower rising channel and breaks to the down side, that is very bearish, short selling the FTSE 100 has proved a profitable trade "

13

Playing footsie

A s bull market trading strategies go, this one takes some beating. It's really simple, too. All you have to do is buy shares in the companies that are being relegated from the FTSE 100 on the day that they drop out of the Index following the FTSE International Committee's Quarterly Index Review, then hold the shares for three

> **❝ you would have made an average quarterly gain of 13.6 per cent on each of the 27 companies that dropped out of the FTSE 100 following the Quarterly Index Review ❞❞**

months before selling up. Then start the process all over again by reinvesting the proceeds into the next laggards being booted out of the blue-chip Index following the next FTSE Committee's Quarterly Index Review.

It may be a simple trade, but it's also one that has reaped hefty gains. In fact, if you had followed this strategy from the beginning of the last equity bull market in March 2003 until the bull run peaked out in June 2007, you would have made an average quarterly gain of 13.6 per cent on each of the

27 companies that dropped out of the FTSE 100 following the Quarterly Index Review (see Table 13.1). By comparison the FTSE 100 Index only managed to rise by 5.3 per cent, on average, in these 13 quarters, giving a very welcome outperformance of 8.4 per cent.

Moreover, the risk:reward of this trade is very favourable. Of the 27 companies dropping out of the FTSE 100, over three-quarters posted a positive return in the three months following their exit from the Index and four of the six losing trades fell by less than 3 per cent. True, shares in two companies posted double digit losses in the quarter after their

table 13.1 Three-month performance of FTSE 100 drop-outs and FTSE 100 from date of expulsion (24 March 2003) to 18 June 2007

FTSE 100 company	Date of expulsion from FTSE 100	Percentage change in share price in following three months (%)	Percentage change in FTSE 100 in following three months (%)	Difference in three-month return between buying share on date of expulsion and FTSE 100 Index (%)
Rolls-Royce	24/03/2003	65.0	11.1	53.9
British Airways	24/03/2003	34.6	11.1	23.5
Royal & Sun Alliance	24/03/2003	50.8	11.1	39.7
Invensys	24/03/2003	50.0	11.1	38.9
Hays	23/06/2003	18.0	4.1	13.9
Capita	23/06/2003	11.5	4.1	7.4
Kelda	22/09/2003	10.5	4.4	6.1
Mitchels & Butler	22/12/2003	11.3	−0.1	11.4
Provident Financial	22/12/2003	17.1	−0.1	17.2
F&C Investment Trust	22/03/2004	−2.3	4.0	−6.3
GKN	21/06/2004	−13.7	1.7	−15.4
Bradford & Bingley	20/09/2004	7.3	2.6	4.7
Tomkins	20/12/2004	9.4	4.1	5.3
Cairn Energy	21/03/2005	23.5	3.1	20.4
Corus Group	20/06/2005	−1.8	6.5	−8.3
Bunzl	20/06/2005	10.9	6.5	4.4
Hays	19/09/2005	0.0	2.2	−2.2
Emap	19/09/2005	1.9	2.2	−0.3
Whitbread	19/12/2005	31.4	8.5	22.9
William Hill	19/12/2005	13.5	8.5	5.0
Daily Mail & General Trust	19/06/2006	−2.3	5.0	−7.3
Cable & Wireless	19/06/2006	14.4	5.0	9.4
Ladbrokes	19/06/2006	1.5	5.0	−3.5
Rentokil Initial	18/09/2006	11.9	6.1	5.8
Schroders	18/09/2006	15.5	6.1	9.4
British Energy	19/12/2006	−19.1	−1.8	−17.3
Cairn Energy	19/03/2007	−2.7	9.8	−12.5
Average		**13.6**	**5.3**	**8.4**

Source: Thomson Reuters Datastream

ejection from the FTSE 100, but even taking those losses into consideration, the trading strategy worked a treat.

Reasons for the phenomenon

I first revealed this trading strategy nine years ago (1999) and have written various articles on the subject since, including 'Playing footsie with the laggards' (2005a) and 'Playing footsie' (2006).

My findings have since been validated by several recent academic studies into the price performance of companies entering and being ejected from the FTSE 100. In a paper – 'Playing footsie with the FTSE 100' (2006) – Professor Jay Dahya, of City University of New York, considered changes to the Index during the period 1984–2003. Professor Dahya noted: 'Deletions to the Index are associated with a negative price response, which is fully reversed over a 120-day period after news of the removal from the index.' He added, 'The rebound in stock prices following exclusion from the FTSE 100 Index is also positively related with analysts' earnings forecasts (upgrades) and negatively related with a change in press coverage.' So less press coverage after these companies leave the Index has no negative effect on their subsequent share price performance, while these companies do seem to benefit from positive analyst coverage following their ejection, which helps the shares to bounce back strongly.

These finding were also confirmed by Brian Mase (2007) of Brunel University. He found that, 'Return reversal around index additions and deletions suggests that buying (selling) pressure moves prices temporarily away from equilibrium.' It is this excessive selling pressure that drives down share prices below fair value and creates the conditions for a bounce back in the shares once the laggards have been ejected.

Technical factors

There are several factors that cause the laggards in the FTSE 100 to bounce back in value after their expulsion from the Index. The most obvious is that they are too cheap following a period of technical selling pressure in the run-up to their expulsion.

Primarily this is due to FTSE 100 Index tracking funds being obliged to sell their shareholdings in companies ejected from the Index, even if they feel that the shares are undervalued. The asset managers simply don't have a choice as the mandate for these tracking funds dictates that they are only allowed to hold shares in constituents of the FTSE 100. This creates systematic selling pressure on companies being deleted from the Index and depresses valuations below what is a fair value.

Second, the FTSE International Committee holds its Quarterly Index Review on the second Wednesday of March, June, September and December, with changes to the Index being implemented seven trading days later. The delay between the announcement of a company's ejection from the Index and the date on which the changes are implemented enables market participants to jump on the bandwagon and profit from this technical selling pressure by fund managers. For instance, some traders will short sell shares they don't own at this time with the aim of trying to make a profit by buying these shares back at a lower price at a later date. In turn, this exacerbates the share price falls of the companies being ejected from the Index.

> **" some traders will short sell shares they don't own with the aim of trying to make a profit by buying these shares back at a lower price at a later date, this exacerbates the share price falls in companies being ejected from the Index "**

Third, the fact that a company is being ejected from the blue-chip Index is also down to a relatively poor share price performance in the previous three months. This creates an additional negative momentum effect, whereby some traders will short sell shares of these underperformers in this period to take advantage of the downward share price momentum, safe in the knowledge that, if the companies are ejected from the Index, there will be additional forced selling by the index tracker funds to drive prices down even lower.

> **" what is interesting is that the downward pressure on the share prices of these laggards seems to peter out at the point the companies are ejected from the FTSE 100, offering the opportunity ... to buy shares on the cheap "**

What is interesting is that the downward pressure on the share prices of these laggards seems to peter out at the point the companies are ejected from the FTSE 100, offering the opportunity for investors in the know to take advantage and buy these shares on the cheap.

Interestingly, the companies promoted to the FTSE 100 to replace the laggards that have been ejected perform less well during their first three months in the Index than they did in the three months leading up to their promotion. Understandably, tracker funds will have been buying these top performers in advance of their promotion, giving the shares a boost, while momentum share traders will have added to this positive price trend by riding on their coat-tails. However, once the companies enter the blue-chip Index, the buying by index tracking funds will start to dry up and momentum traders are likely to focus their attention on the next group of companies likely to be promoted to the FTSE 100.

The mechanics of the FTSE 100 Quarterly Review

Entry to the FTSE 100 Index is based on market value of the constituents. The rules used by the FTSE International Committee at its Quarterly Review state that inclusion in the FTSE 100 Index is automatic if a company in the FTSE 250 Index has a market value that places it in 90th position or above in the FTSE 100. A company is automatically excluded from the FTSE 100 at the Quarterly Review if its market value reaches the 111th position or below.

> **❝ academic studies and the evidence from the last bull market support the case that the laggards are ripe for a re-rating when they are ejected from the FTSE 100 Index ❞**

As a result of these rules – and in an effort to reduce excessive turnover of stocks into and out of the Index – the FTSE 100 Index comprises the largest 90 companies by market capitalisation plus 10 of the next 20 largest companies.

In addition, there is a reserve list of six companies that are the highest-ranking non-Index constituent stocks at the close of business prior to the Quarterly Review date. Those companies will be promoted to the Index between the Quarterly Review dates if a constituent drops out in the interim period. This could occur due to a takeover, delisting or demerger of a constituent company.

trading strategy 30

Buy laggards the day they are ejected from the Index

Academic studies and the evidence from the last bull market support the case that the laggards are ripe for a re-rating when they are ejected from the FTSE 100 Index. However, remember that this is a bull market phenomenon, as recent evidence indicates that companies ejected have performed very poorly during the 2007/2008 bear market (see next page on bear markets blues).

▶

The clear trading strategy is to buy the laggards on the day they are ejected from the FTSE 100 Index following the FTSE International Committee's Quarterly Review and hold the shares for three months (full details of companies being ejected from the Index are available at **www.ftse.com/Indices** – the announcement of these changes are available on the website on the second Wednesday of March, June, September and December).

Bear market blues

During the 2007/2008 UK equity bear market companies being ejected from the FTSE 100 have shown a clear tendency to underperform the benchmark Index in the quarter after being ejected from the Index (see Table 13.2).

In fact, of the 14 companies ejected from the FTSE 100 at the FTSE International Quarterly Reviews between June 2007 (when the UK bull market peaked) and June 2008, only four shares managed to generate a significant positive return in the following three months. On average, shares in those 14 companies fell by 14 per cent in the 3-month period after leaving the FTSE 100 against a 7.9 per cent fall in the Index.

The common theme among these companies has been downward pressure on earnings. For instance, mortgage bank Bradford & Bingley has suffered from tighter conditions in the money markets for funding in the credit crisis; housebuilder Taylor Woodrow has felt the impact of a slowdown in the housing market on both sides of the Atlantic; while telephone directory group Yell, retailing giant DSG and support services group Rentokil all issued profit warnings after being ejected from the Index.

It is worth noting, though, that an increase in profit warnings and earnings disappointments are normal occurrences in bear markets as they have historically been associated with periods of earnings recession. So, instead of shares in these bear market laggards getting a boost from earnings upgrades, as Mr Dahya found in his study, the negative share price trends prior to their ejection from the FTSE 100 have been acerbated by earnings downgrades. In that sense, their subsequent poor share price performance following their ejection from the Index is quite rational.

table 13.2 Three-month performance of FTSE 100 drop-outs and FTSE 100 from date of expulsion (18 June 2007) to 23 June 2008

FTSE 100 company	Date of expulsion from FTSE 100	Percentage change in share price in following three months (%)	Percentage change in FTSE 100 in following three months (%)	Difference in three-month return between buying share on date of expulsion and FTSE 100 Index (%)
Bradford & Bingley	18/06/2007	−29.2	−2.1	−27.1
Kelda	24/09/2007	26.0	−0.4	26.4
Segro	24/09/2007	−10.7	−0.4	−10.3
Drax	24/09/2007	0.3	−0.4	0.7
Punch Taverns	24/12/2007	−33.8	−14.6	−19.2
Tate & Lyle	24/12/2007	24.3	−14.6	38.9
Daily Mail & General Trust	24/12/2007	−12.7	−14.6	1.9
DSG International	24/12/2007	−41.0	−14.6	−26.4
Mitchells & Butlers	24/12/2007	−24.3	−14.6	−9.7
Barratt Developments	24/12/2007	−12.8	−14.6	1.8
Northern Rock	24/12/2007	5.3	−14.6	19.9
Taylor Wimpey	25/03/2008	−61.9	−1.5	−60.4
Rentokil Initial	25/03/2008	14.8	−1.5	16.3
Yell Group	25/03/2008	−40.5	−1.5	−39.0
Average		−14.0	−7.9	−6.2

Source: Thomson Reuters Datastream

The message, though, is clear: do not try and buy the laggards in bear markets as other factors, such as earnings disappointments, are likely to dampen the enthusiasm of investors looking for a rebound in the share prices of those companies dropping out of the FTSE 100. Moreover, bear markets are associated with long periods of negative investor sentiment and greater risk aversion as investors try to protect their capital, so any earnings disappointment in bear markets is likely to be severely punished, as the examples above clearly prove.

❝ the message is clear: do not try and buy the laggards in bear markets ❞

chapter

14

Days like these

Sometimes the stock market behaves rather oddly on certain days of the year. It therefore pays to know when this could happen and, more importantly, how to profit from such apparent market anomalies.

Friday the 13th – lucky for some

Friday the 13th has a long history of being seen as an unfavourable day, not least in the Judaeo-Christian world. If investors are superstitious, too, then this could impact returns from the stock market when the 13th day of the month falls on a Friday. Fortunately, the mood of investors does not appear to take a superstitious turn for the worse on these days at all. In fact, a series of academic studies have shown that returns are actually significantly *higher* when the 13th day of the month falls on a Friday.

For instance, Terence Mills and Andrew Coutts (1995) showed that the UK market has posted a higher return on Friday 13th than all other Fridays for the period 1986–1992. These findings were confirmed four years later when Mr Coutts (1999) examined the performance of the FT 30 Index for the period 1935–1994.

In 2002, academic Brian Lucey of the University of Dublin extended the study beyond the UK stock market to see whether or not this was an international phenomenon. In his paper Mr Lucey (2002) looked at the performance of the FTSE World Indices for 19 countries between January 1988 and March 2000 – a period that included 698 Fridays, of which 23 fell on the 13th.

Mr Lucey discovered that, when the 13th day of the month fell on a Friday, returns on those days in 11 of the 19 countries were statistically significantly higher compared to other normal Fridays. Countries where returns were greater include Germany, Ireland, Italy, Japan, Holland, Norway, Spain, Sweden and the UK. In fact, the size of the difference in returns from those stock markets was, in some cases, 10 times greater on Friday 13th than on other Fridays.

> **academic studies have shown that returns are actually significantly *higher* when the 13th day of the month falls on a Friday**

This may be hard to understand because there is no apparent reason, empirical or theoretical, to suggest that Fridays falling on the 13th should generate better returns, but they undoubtedly have done so in the past and, importantly, continue to do so. Indeed, in the UK, the FTSE 100 rose by 0.3 per cent and 0.7 per cent, respectively, on Friday 13 July and Friday 13 April 2007 – the only two days that year there was a Friday 13th. Also, true to form, the FTSE 100 rose by 0.2 per cent on Friday 13 June 2008 – the only day in 2008 when the 13th day of the month was a Friday. To put these rises in perspective, in the past 24 years, the average return on other Fridays has been less than 0.1 per cent.

Reasons for the phenomenon

It would be easy to conclude that this phenomenon is nothing more than the result of data mining by academics. However, the evidence of the studies – none of which, admittedly, has given an explanation for this extraordinary effect – clearly shows that the Friday 13th effect occurs across many different international stock markets and has produced significantly above average returns. Moreover, the data samples in these studies have been substantial and cover a long period of time.

> **evidence clearly shows that the Friday 13th effect occurs across many different international stock markets and has produced significantly above average returns**

One explanation – specific to the UK market – is that, historically, share prices have produced good returns on Friday. This is partly down to a weekend effect – that is, companies are more likely to release good news ahead of the weekend, boosting their share prices, as a way to capitalise on the fact that investors will have both Saturday and Sunday (non-trading days on the UK stock market) to digest this news. For the same reason, companies are less likely to release bad news on Friday as this is more likely to get greater press coverage over the weekend when there is less corporate news flow for the media to report due to the stock market being closed. Also, in the UK, there are fewer company results released on Fridays than any other day of the week, so there is less chance of poor corporate news denting sentiment and weighing down share prices.

Therefore, the fact that the market rises when a Friday falls on the 13th day of the month should not be that surprising. However, this fails to explain why returns on Friday *13th* are so significantly above the average for this day of the week. Although we can't explain this trend, we can nonetheless profit from it.

trading strategy 31

Profit from the Friday the 13th effect

Given that Fridays have historically produced the better returns than any other day of the week, and these have been higher than normal when the 13th day of the month falls on a Friday, then the obvious way to profit from this phenomenon is to buy a FTSE 100 index tracker fund shortly before the close of trading on Thursday when the following day is the 13th day of the month. Look to take profits by the close of trading on the Friday.

ETFs that track the performance of the FTSE 100 Index include those issued by Lyxor (TIDM: L100), a subsidiary of French investment bank Société Générale, Deutsche Bank (TIDM: XUKX) and Barclays iShares (TIDM: ISF). These ETFs are traded in the same way as ordinary shares and have the additional benefit of being exempt from UK stamp duty when purchased.

Alternatively, place an up spread bet on the FTSE 100 through a spread betting firm shortly before the close of trading on Thursday when the following Friday falls on the 13th. Look to take profits by the close of trading on the Friday. Spread betting firms in the UK include IG Index, City Index, CMC Markets and Cantor Index and you can place a bet for as little as £1 per point movement in the FTSE 100 Index.

One final way to benefit from the tendency of the UK market to rise on Friday 13th is to place a fixed odds bet that the FTSE 100 Index will rise on that day. Fixed odds betting websites (such as www.extrabet.com) offer the option to bet on whether the UK market will rise or fall on every day of the trading week. The optimum strategy is to place a bet that the UK market will rise on Friday 13th shortly after the market closes on Thursday afternoon. The bet can be closed out at any time during the trading day and will be settled at the close of trading on Friday.

In 2009, there are three days when the 13th day of the month falls on a Friday: 13 February, 13 March and 13 November. In the following years, it falls in August 2010, May 2011, January 2012, April 2012 and July 2012.

“ in 2009, there are three days when the 13th day of the month falls on a Friday: 13 February, 13 March and 13 November; in the following years, it falls in August 2010, May 2011, January 2012, April 2012 and July 2012 ”

15

S&P 500 dog effect

This is possibly one of the simplest investment strategies ever devised. It is also one of the most profitable. Here is what you need to do.

On 1 October each year, buy the ten worst-performing stocks in the S&P 500 Index of US stocks based on their price performance for the previous three years. Hold these shares for only three months, until 31 December, then sell them. That's it.

You don't even have to pore over the finer details of fundamental analysis used by stockbrokers and equity analysts when deciding on the ten shares to hold. So, forget about dividend yields, price to earnings multiples and price to book values (the ratio of a company's market value to its net asset value). This strategy does not rely on any of those valuation measures to work – and work it certainly does.

If you had followed this strategy during the past decade, you would have turned in an average quarterly gain of 23 per cent (see Table 15.1). That is over 15 percentage points more than a S&P 500 Index tracker made in the final 3 months of the year.

So why does this trading strategy, of buying the worst-performing stocks in the S&P 500 Index, work so well?

table 15.1 S&P 500 dog portfolios – performance from 1 October to 31 December

Year	Performance of ten losers from previous three years (%)	S&P 500 performance (%)
1997	2.3	2.6
1998	41.8	20.8
1999	10.4	14.6
2000	4.7	−8.1
2001	37.2	10.3
2002	55.4	7.9
2003	27.1	11.7
2004	34.1	8.7
2005	15.5	1.5
2006	5.5	6.2
Average	23.4	7.6

Source: Thomson Reuters Datastream

Reasons for the phenomenon

Shares overreact to news

In a now famous paper, academics Werner De Bondt and Richard Thaler (1987) found that portfolios consisting of the 35 worst-performing stocks in the S&P 500 (using price data for the previous three years) out-performed the 35 best-performing stocks by an average of 25 per cent in the subsequent three years for each three-year period between 1933 and 1979. They (De Bondt and Thaler, 1987; Thompson and Dillow, 2003) noted at the time, 'Most people overreact to unexpected and dramatic news events. And you can make big money by exploiting this.'

> **most people overreact to unexpected and dramatic news events, you can make big money by exploiting this**

For instance, some companies get a bad reputation for perennially disappointing and, as a result, both shareholders and potential new investors are more inclined to ignore the few merits the company and its management have. In the most extreme cases, where share prices of the worst performers in the S&P 500 have fallen by over 90 per cent during a 3-year period – as has been the case for the majority of the 10 stocks included in these dog portfolios in the past – this savage derating can take valuations way below what is a fair value.

So why does a policy of buying on 1 October do so well? Why not pick any other date? Fortunately, there are some very rational explanations why the policy of buying the worst-performing stocks on this specific date works so well.

Window dressing

The reasons the dogs of the S&P 500 start to bounce back on 1 October is easy to explain: the US fiscal year ends on 30 September. At that time, US fund managers must send reports to their investors detailing their performance during the year. However, the last thing they want to put in those reports is the fact that they are holding some of the worst-performing shares in the S&P 500. It would hardly inspire confidence in their stock-picking ability if shareholders in their funds found out that they had taken big hits on some of the Rottweilers in the Index.

As a result, in an effort to hoodwink their own shareholders that they're better stock-pickers than they really are, the asset managers sell the dog stocks before the fiscal year end. Other fund managers, who have the same motives, are reluctant to buy them.

> **why the dogs start to bounce back on 1 October is easy to explain: the US fiscal year ends on 30 September; the upshot is that loser stocks are especially undervalued at the end of September, so are ripe for bouncing back**

The upshot is that loser stocks are likely to be especially undervalued at the end of September, so are ripe for bouncing back, which is when the 'buy-the-dog' investment strategy kicks in.

There is certainly some merit in this explanation, although it does assume that enough investors are stupid enough to be taken in by this window dressing ruse. Moreover, it also assumes that less savvy investors haven't learned that stocks overreact on the downside in this way. Otherwise, they would simply buy the loser stocks, which would push their prices up and so make it impossible for other later investors to make money from them.

Even if we accept that the window dressing ruse exacerbates the downward pressure on share prices in the months leading up to 30 September, it is very unlikely that it can be the *only* reason for stocks then performing so strongly in the following three months. Instead, there's an alternative explanation. It's all to do with risk.

Risk

Stocks that have fallen by 90 per cent or more in the past 3 years carry loads of risk. There are five types of risk.

- *Volatility* Stocks that have fallen by 90 per cent or more can fall by another 90 per cent – that's basic arithmetic. The fact that they have fallen so far is evidence that they are more volatile than most stocks and so have more chance of falling another 90 per cent – that's basic statistics. So, these dog shares are likely to be more volatile than the average constituent of the S&P 500. Bear in mind, too, that stocks can be just as volatile on the up side, when bouncing back, as they are when falling.

> **stocks can be just as volatile on the up side, when bouncing back, as they are when falling**

- *Liquidity risk* The ten worst dog stocks in the S&P 500 have low absolute prices. That often means they have bigger bid–offer spreads (the difference between the prices market makers offer to buy or sell at) than most stocks. As a result, it costs more to trade them. In turn, this means that, if things go wrong and investors are forced to sell up, that could be very expensive indeed. Liquidity risk works both ways, however. On the down side, it depresses share prices and sometimes forces them below fair value, but on the up side, liquidity risk falls as prices rise, offering scope for above-average price rises when the stocks start to bounce back.

- *Distress risk* Dog stocks that plunge by 90 per cent or more run a far greater risk of going bust than other stocks. For one, they usually carry much higher levels of balance sheet gearing (the ratio of net borrowings to the net assets of the company) than the average constituent in the S&P 500. In some cases, the bank covenants on the debt will be related to the market capitalisation of the company, so, the further the stock falls, the greater the risk of a breach of these covenants. Moreover, investors clearly sense this, as distress risk will be an increasing factor in the downwards share price momentum seen in poorly performing stocks. If investor sentiment improves, however, and the perception of a company going bust or breaching its bank covenants diminishes – which is likely to be the case if the stocks start to rise strongly – then distress risk falls, too, which, in turn, helps the stock price bounce back.

- *Market risk* The fact that the ten worst-performing dog stocks have fallen so much at the same time (in most cases the falls have been far greater than falls on the S&P 500) means that they have a high sensitivity to market moves. That is another source of risk, but one that helps the dog stocks rise faster than the market when they bounce back.

- *Economic risk* Dog stocks are generally in cyclical sectors, which have in the past done well during winter months. That is because winter is a dangerous time for the economy. Academics have estimated that half of the ordinary business cycle is the result of seasonal swings in output around Christmas time. Cyclical stocks – including dogs of the S&P 500 – offer high returns in winter to compensate investors for this risk. Common sense tells us that risky stocks should outperform other stocks eventually, simply to compensate for their greater risk. The combination of the US fiscal year end, window dressing by fund managers and the start of a seasonally good time to be holding equities (the S&P 500 Index has risen by 4.4 per cent, on average, in the final three months of the year since 1950) all helps these risky stocks to outperform in the final quarter.

> ❝ common sense tells us that risky stocks should outperform other stocks eventually, simply to compensate for their greater risk ❞

Risk and reward

The dog stocks may have their day in the final quarter of the year, but don't expect the recovery to be a long-lasting one.

It used to be the case that you could just buy the dog stocks on 1 October and hold them for a year to reap even bigger returns. This certainly worked between 1996 and 2003 (see Table 15.2). In recent years, however, investors trying to bet on sustained share price recoveries by holding the 10 dog stocks for a full 12 months have been bitterly disappointed. In fact, in the 12 months to end September 2004, 2005, 2006 and 2007, that strategy would have lost you money. Even worse, in each of those years, the S&P 500 recorded decent gains so the ten shares performed very poorly in a rising market (see Table 15.2).

Interestingly, an analysis of all the dog portfolios since 1996 shows that they have one thing in common: there is a clear bias for the best of the gains to come in the four-month period between 1 October and 31 January. For instance, if you had bought the ten worst-performing stocks in the S&P 500 (on the basis of their share price performance for the previous three years) on 1 October 2003 and held them until 31 December,

table 15.2 S&P 500 dog portfolio – performance for 12-month period

Year ending 30 September	Performance of ten losers from previous three years (%)	S&P 500 performance (%)
1996	141.6	21.6
1997	79.6	40.5
1998	32.6	9.4
1999	191.4	29.0
2000	67.2	15.4
2001	61.6	−29.8
2002	−21.7	−21.5
2003	176.0	22.0
2004	−4.9	12.0
2005	−2.6	10.2
2006	−1.4	8.6
2007	−4.5	14.2
Average	**59.6**	**11.0**

Source: Thomson Reuters Datastream

you would have made a very healthy 27.1 per cent return. If you had held on another three weeks, until 20 January, however, you would have more than doubled your return to 59.5 per cent (see Table 15.3). Remember, that return was reaped in just 16 weeks. It's worth noting, though, that it was as good as it got as the 10 dogs started to bite, not bark, for the rest of the year, ending 30 September 2004 down 4.9 per cent for the 12 months (see Table 15.2).

It was a similar story a year later (see Table 15.4). The 10 dog stocks that year stormed ahead, notching up a hefty 34.1 per cent gain in the 3 months to end December 2004. By 30 September 2005, however, those 10 stocks had given up all the gains made and ended the year down 2.6 per cent overall, dragged down by the dire subsequent performances of Delta Airlines and Winn-Dixie Stores, both of which eventually went bust.

❝ in 2005, the dog portfolio was up by 15.5 per cent in the 3 months to 31 December ❞

In 2005, the ten dog stocks that had performed so dismally in the previous three years roared ahead once more in the final quarter of that year, buoyed up by double digit gains from the likes of drug giant Merck and insurance group March & McClellan (see Table 15.5).

table 15.3 S&P 500 dog portfolio 2003 – performance from 1 October 2003 to 20 January 2004

S&P 500 companies	TIDM	Share price ($) 30 September 2003	Share price ($) high 20 January 2004	Percentage change (%) to high
Lucent Technologies	LU	2.16	4.75	119.9
PMC-Sierra	PMCS	13.19	24.51	85.8
Sun Microsystems	SUNW	3.31	5.62	69.8
Applied Micro Circuits	AMCC	4.86	7.86	61.7
JDS Uniphase	JDSU	3.60	5.73	59.2
ADC Telecom	ADCT	2.33	3.60	54.5
Siebel Systems	SEBL	9.76	14.13	44.8
Dynegy 'A'	DYN	3.60	5.15	43.1
Qwest Communications	Q	3.40	4.43	30.3
Ciena	CIEN	5.86	7.41	26.5
Average				**59.5**
S&P 500		1018	1139	11.9

Source: Thomson Reuters Datastream

table 15.4 S&P 500 dog portfolio 2004 – performance from 1 October 2004 to 31 December 2004

Company	TIDM	Share price ($) 30 September 2004	Share price ($) 31 December 2004	Percentage change (%)
Delta Air Lines	DAL	3.29	7.48	127.4
Ciena	CIEN	1.98	3.31	67.2
Winn-Dixie Stores	WIN	3.09	4.55	47.2
Calpine	CPN	2.90	3.94	35.9
Qwest	Q	3.33	4.44	33.3
Electronic Data Systems	EDS	19.39	23.10	19.1
El Paso	EP	9.19	10.40	13.2
King Pharmaceuticals	KG	11.94	12.40	3.9
Tenet Healthcare	THC	10.79	10.98	1.8
Dynegy A	DYN	4.99	4.62	−7.4
Average				**34.1**
S&P 500		1114	1212	8.8

Source: Thomson Reuters Datastream

The dog portfolio was up by 15.5 per cent in the 3 months to 31 December 2005, handsomely outperforming the meagre 1.5 per cent rise of the S&P 500 Index. As in 2004, though, this was a very good time to bank profits, with the 2005 dog portfolio ending the 12 months to 30 September 2006 down 1.4 per cent. This was not helped by Dana Corporation entering Chapter 11 Bankruptcy Protection in March 2006, which, again, highlights how the bumper gains being made are a reflection of the high risks these portfolios carry.

In 2006, the dogs fared less well – rising 5.5 per cent in the final quarter of the year against a 6.2 per cent rise in the S&P 500 Index (see Table 15.6). This did, however, maintain the record at 10 years on the trot that the S&P 500 dog portfolios have returned a positive return in the final quarter of the year having been the worst performers in the S&P 500 Index in the previous three years, giving a 100 per cent track record.

table 15.5 S&P 500 dog portfolio 2005 – performance from 1 October 2005 to 31 December 2005

Company	Percentage change in final quarter of 2005 (%)
Fifth Third Bancorp	39.1
Marsh & McLennan	30.5
Merck	29.2
New York Times 'A'	27.7
Family Dollar stores	22.6
Interpublic	10.1
Big Lots	9.3
Tenet Healthcare	8.5
Delphi	0.6
Dana	−22.7
Average	**15.5**
S&P 500	1.5

Source: Thomson Reuters Datastream

table 15.6 S&P 500 dog portfolio 2006 – performance from 1 October 2006 to 31 December 2006

Company	Percentage change in final quarter of 2006 (%)
Unisys	38.5
Boston Scientific	16.2
PMC-Sierra	13.0
Marsh & McLennan	8.9
New York Times 'A'	6.0
Solectron	0.0
Watson Pharmaceuticals	−0.5
JDS Uniphase	−4.9
Sanmina-Sci	−7.8
Tenet Healthcare	−14.4
Average	**5.5**
S&P 500	6.2

Source: Thomson Reuters Datastream

trading strategy 32

Utilise the S&P 500 dog effect

It's worth remembering that dog portfolios only offer the prospect of substantial returns *because* they carry significant risks, as the bankruptcies of Delta Airlines and Winn-Dixie confirm.

That said, there is a clear bias for the worst-performing stocks in the S&P 500 in the three years to end of September to start to bounce back in the first three months after recording this dire performance. So, if you can stomach the above-average risks associated with this type of trade, buying these shares on 1 October each year with the intention of banking profits three months later is the advised strategy.

If you want to ride your luck a bit longer, running these portfolios into January has more often than not paid dividends in the past. Be warned, though, be quick to take the profits as these bumper gains have quickly disappeared in the past four years, leaving the dog portfolios showing a loss, not a profit, after 12 months.

The easiest way to buy S&P 500 stocks is through a UK stockbroker that offers trading on US stocks. Execution of the share trades is done in the same way as for

UK shares. Please note that there is a five-hour time difference between New York and London and the New York Stock Exchange only opens at 2.30 p.m. GMT.

Alternatively, the large spread betting firms in the UK – IG Index, City Index, CMC Markets and Cantor Index – offer trading in the shares of most S&P 500 companies. There are several advantages to investing in this way. First, there is no foreign exchange risk as you can place an up bet in sterling for every cent movement in the dollar share price of a US stock. Second, profits are tax free as spread betting is not currently subject to UK capital gains tax.

chapter

16

Dogs of the FTSE All-Share Index

Petlovers attracted to the S&P 500 dog effect described in the last chapter may also be interested in the UK breed of this equity dog effect. It's just as simple and just as profitable.

In December each year, buy shares in the ten worst performers in the FTSE All-Share Index, based on their share price performance in the previous three years. At the end of January, sell these shares. That's it.

There is no need to do any high-brow investment analysis at all because, like the S&P 500 dog effect, there are specific reasons behind these UK dog shares putting in a Crufts-worthy performance after behaving so badly during the previous three years. These shares most certainly have their day between December and the end of January, posting an average gain of 18.3 per cent each year between 1993 and 2003.

This stellar share price outperformance has continued in recent years, with the portfolio of the 10 worst-performing shares in the FTSE All-Share Index from the previous three years rising in value by 23.4 per cent

> there are specific reasons behind these UK dog shares putting in a Crufts-worthy performance after behaving so badly during the previous three years

between December 2003 and January 2004. One year later, the next portfolio of the worst 10 poor performers in the Index (selected by their share price performances for the period December 2001 to December 2004) had a swift rebound in fortunes, rising by 11.9 per cent between December 2004 and January 2005. It was a similar story in 2006 when the 10 dog shares in the Index (selected by their performance for the period

December 2002 to December 2005) rose by an average of 13.6 per cent between December 2005 and January 2006. Further, although the 2007 portfolio of 10 dog shares (selected by their performance for the period December 2003 to December 2006) only managed a 6.5 per cent rise between mid-December and the end of January 2007, it was, appropriately, a dogged performance as the FTSE All-Share fell by 0.5 per cent in the same period (see Table 16.1).

table 16.1 Performance of FTSE All-Share dog shares between mid-December and January

Year	Performance of FTSE All-Share dog shares between mid-December and January, 2004–2007
2004	23.4
2005	11.9
2006	13.6
2007	6.5

Source: *Investors Chronicle*

Reasons for the phenomenon

In contrast to the US, there have been very few academic studies into why previously badly performing shares in the UK should outperform the Index so dramatically. However, one study, by Glen Arnold and Rose Baker of Salford Business School (2007), looked into this phenomenon over the period 1960–2002, they concluded that:

An investment strategy of buying a portfolio of the loser shares outperforms one buying the winner shares and also outperforms the UK market consistently over a long period. The evidence supports the view that there are systematic valuation errors in the stock market caused by investor overreaction.

❝❝ an investment strategy of buying a portfolio of the loser shares outperforms one buying the winner shares ❞❞

However, this investor overreaction, selling down shares way below fair value, reverses itself over time. The study found that the portfolio of loser stocks (from the previous five years) outperforms the market by 8.9 per cent a year in the following 5-year period.

Investor overreaction

Investor preference and bias is another factor driving shares of the winning and losing stocks far above and below their equilibrium value. Arnold and Baker (2007) noted that, 'Investors as a group develop an unreasonable preference for winners ... because they try and extrapolate past share price performance even when such trends are unlikely to persist.' Consequently, this preference for chasing winning stocks pushes their prices above the fair value justified by fundamentals, while those stocks out of favour are driven down way below their fair value. They added, 'Investors equate good companies (those with good management, earnings and strong market positions) with good shares, thus bidding the prices of the winners excessively, while ignoring the so-called dogs.'

Investor psychology

Investor psychology also plays its part in creating the conditions whereby the dog shares bounce back after performing so badly for so long as poor-performing stocks will have previously been shunned by asset managers. For instance, it is far easier for fund managers to justify their stock selection to superiors if a company has been performing well and is well-known. By contrast shares in companies that have fallen heavily in the past will carry far higher risks. The academics found that one in eight of the losing stocks from the previous five years went bust in the subsequent five-year period. Arnold and Baker (2007) noted that:

> **" fund managers are often led to believe that it is better to fail conventionally than to succeed unconventionally "**

A fund manager would be perceived as countenancing too much risk in advancing the case for investing in a series of the loser stocks. Fund managers are often led to believe that it is better to fail conventionally than to succeed unconventionally.

High risks, high returns

Make no mistake, the risks of this strategy are very real and no different from those affecting the S&P 500 dogs: volatility, distress, market, economic and liquidity risks (see Chapter 15). Distress risk is very important as a high percentage of the companies that have seen their share prices plunge during the previous few years will have weaker balance sheets. In some cases, accumulated tax losses from past periods of poor trading may have completely wiped out shareholders' funds. That makes it more difficult for such companies to borrow and more expensive, too. So, the high rewards investors have earned by buying the dog shares is, to some extent, a reflection of the greater risk they are taking on.

Bounce back effect

The fact that the dogs eventually bounce back has not been lost on readers of *Investors Chronicle* magazine (Green, 2007). So why is a strategy of buying these shares specifically in mid-December and holding on to them until the end of January so profitable?

First, fund managers are tempted to de-risk their portfolios to some extent at the end of the year by locking in performance and banking profits. That is understandable as their bonuses are likely to be dependent on their fund's performance during the past calendar year. This de-risking not only works for their better holdings, but there could be a temptation to overdo the selling and get rid of some of their risky shareholdings, too.

❝ fund managers are tempted to overdo the selling and get rid of some of their risky shareholdings ❞

In turn, this gives these shares a chance to bounce back in January. In addition, there does seem to be an appetite for risky stocks in January as fund managers, whose performance is being judged on a calendar year basis, are more prepared to buy these shares at this time as they have a whole 12 months to rectify any investment mistakes they make at the start of the year.

Second, there is also a December effect that has an impact on movements in the constituent companies of the FTSE Small Cap, FTSE Fledgling and FTSE All-Small indices. Unlike the blue-chip FTSE 100 and mid-cap FTSE 250, which have Quarterly Index Reviews (see Chapter 13), there is only *one* review for constituents of these small cap indices. That review takes place on the second Wednesday of December, with changes to the indices being implemented seven trading days later.

So, if the FTSE Policy Group decide at their annual meeting in December that some of the worst-performing shares will be relegated from the Index they are constituents of, fund managers who track the smaller cap indices – and can only hold shares in the constituent members – will have no choice but to sell their shareholdings. This technical and forced selling pressure ends around seven to ten days before the end of December, offering scope for investors to buy shares in these companies on the cheap. This again helps the dog shares to bounce back in January.

Utilise the FTSE All-Share Index dog effect

Make no mistake, buying UK dog shares, even on a short-term basis, is a high-risk trade. On the up side, it is one that has generated significant gains for the past 15 years. Remember, too, that those double digit gains are being made in a very short space of time – generally from mid-December to the end of January.

If you can stomach the risk, then buying a portfolio of the dog shares in the FTSE All-Share Index in mid-December and holding them for six weeks is a decent strategy. Every year, *Investors Chronicle* analyses the share price performance of the worst fallers in the Index over the past three years and publishes a list of the ten dog shares to buy in mid-December. The FTSE All-Share consists of around 910 companies, including those in the blue-chip FTSE 100, the mid cap FTSE 250 and the FTSE small cap indices. The only proviso is that the market capitalisation of the companies in the dog portfolios is a minimum of £50 million.

It is important to buy shares in all *ten* companies as some may fall in value, but, in the past, such losses have been offset by gains made by some of the risers. It is also worth noting that, tempting as it is to run your profits beyond the end of January, some of the companies *will* go bust. Solvency risk is a risk too far for many investors and it is why the least risky and recommended strategy is to buy the ten dog shares in mid-December and hold them for six weeks only.

"buying UK dog shares is a high-risk trade, on the up side, it is one that has generated significant gains"

Budgeting for profit

The Chancellor of the Exchequer has his moment of glory in the House of Commons twice a year. First, in the autumn, the government's spending and tax-raising plans are unveiled in the Pre-Budget Report, but that is only the appetiser to the main course. The Chancellor serves up the Budget in March, revealing the full details of his plans to the nation.

Politics may be a minefield, but, thankfully, the stock markets are far more predictable in the way that they react to the Budget. That is good news because it means that we can profit by being politically correct with how we play the markets at that time of the year.

> **" on Budget day the stock market has risen 75 per cent of the time since 1945; the odds of making a profit on Budget day improve even more by analysing how share prices moved in the five trading days before Budget day "**

Budget day and the stock market

It may be a little-known fact, but share prices generally react favourably on Budget day, rising an incredible 75 per cent of the time in the past 65 Budgets since World War II. True to form, the UK stock market knotched up gains on Budget day in the past 3 years, rising by 1.6 per cent in March 2008, 0.7 per cent in 2007 and 0.3 per cent in 2006. That long-term record is a solid enough reason on its own to buy shares on the eve of Budget day, but it is not the only one.

In fact, the tendency for the market to rise on Budget day is actually very sensible. It can be seen either as a relief rally by financial markets, for there are no fiscal skeletons in the government's cupboard, or, if the news is rather good for companies, taxpayers and the economy, investors will react favourably by marking up share prices.

In effect, by buying shares just ahead of Budget day, you are betting that there will be no nasty surprises in the Chancellor's speech that could unsettle the financial markets. The history books show that this is a rare occurrence indeed.

Pre-Budget trading signals

Fortunately, we can increase the odds of making a profit on Budget day by looking at how prices move in the five trading days prior to the Budget. Research by stock market historian David Schwartz (2006b) shows that share price movements in the range of –0.7 per cent to 0.9 per cent in this 5-day trading period are a great predictor that the stock market will rise on Budget day.

> **“ since 1944, there have been 26 occasions when the UK market moved ahead of the Budget; it went on to rise on Budget Day itself in no fewer than 23 of those years ””**

In fact, since 1944, there have been 26 occasions when the UK market moved in this range ahead of the Budget. It went on to rise on Budget day itself in no fewer than 23 of those years. The two near misses involved miniscule losses in 1995 and 2001, worth less than 5 points on the FTSE 100 Index.

The market last rose in this five-day trading range in 2006 and, true to form, investors buying the FTSE 100 Index on the eve of the Budget were rewarded with a 0.3 per cent gain in the index on Budget day.

Reasons for the phenomenon

The fact that investors react so positively to the Budget when share prices move in this five-day trading period is easy to explain. Bullish, but not overly extended, share price rises ahead of Budget day indicate investor optimism and this positive momentum can easily carry through to Budget day. Equally, if share prices have marked time or made modest losses ahead of the Budget – indicating nervousness by investors – then, assuming that there are no unpleasant surprises on the day itself, they are likely to greet the Budget positively as this risk aversion is likely to have been overdone.

Take advantage of Budget day optimism

The first trading strategy is to buy the FTSE 100 Index shortly before the close of trading the day before Budget day to take advantage of the near 90 per cent chance that share prices will rise on Budget day itself if they have moved in the range −0.7 per cent to 0.9 per cent in the previous 5-day trading period. At the end of trading on Budget day, close out the trade and bank profits if all has gone to plan. It then pays to monitor how the market behaves on the day after the Budget (see Post-Budget trading rules below).

Post-Budget trading rules

We can also make money in the weeks following the Budget just by following a few hard and fast rules, as share price movements on Budget day and the following day have great predictive powers for the future performance of the UK market.

Mr Schwartz (2006b) also found that small swings in the stock market on Budget day and the following day are a bad omen for the performance of share prices for the 14 trading days after that.

In the past 38 years, there have been 17 occasions when the UK market moved in the range of −0.5 per cent to 0.9 per cent on Budget day and the next day. Remarkably, 14 trading days later, share prices were lower in all bar two of those 17 years.

❝ small swings in the stock market on Budget day and the following day are a bad omen for the 14 trading days after that ❞

It's worth noting that the only two exceptions were in 1983 and 1989, when share prices rose by a modest 0.6 per cent in this subsequent 14-day trading period. So, if history is any guide, small movements in share prices across these two days are a leading indicator to short sell the market during the following 14 trading days (see page 145 on mechanics of trading the UK market).

Reasons for the phenomenon

Investors react quickly to the government's announcement and small price movements of this order suggest that, at best, they are moderately happy, but not overwhelmingly so, with the Budget, while small share price falls suggests that they are probably pretty neutral about it. Both of these scenarios are hardly a bullish case for buying shares.

This trend proved itself once again in March 2008, with share price gains on Budget day being wiped out by similarly sized falls on the day after, leaving investors no better placed than when they started. Fast forward three weeks and the market had dropped by 1.15 per cent in the course of 14 trading days. In 2006, it was a similar story, with a flattish performance around Budget day being a precursor to modest falls during the next 14 trading days.

trading strategy 35

Take advantage of post-Budget falls

If prices have moved in the range of −0.5 per cent to 0.9 per cent on Budget day and the following day, it is the cue to short sell the FTSE 100 through a spread bet to profit from the likely fall in share prices in the following 14 trading days. Look to close out this position after 14 trading days.

Remember, in the past four decades, when the UK stock market has performed in this way, there has been a near 90 per cent chance that it will be lower at the end of that 14-day trading period.

Post-Budget trading rules

Mr Schwartz (2006b) has also noted that, when share prices move markedly in one direction or another (outside the range of −0.5 per cent to 0.9 per cent) on Budget day and the following day, it is a great signal that the market will be higher 14 trading days later. For instance, the UK stock market surged ahead by 1.1 per cent on those days in March 2007, giving a major buying signal to investors. The Index then rose by 1.7 per cent in the course of the next 14 trading days, boosting the coffers of investors privy to these little-known trading patterns. It was not a one-off event either, as there have been 22 years since 1970 when the UK market has either risen by more than 0.9 per cent or fallen by more than 0.5 per cent on Budget day and the day after. Amazingly, 90 per cent of the time, the FTSE All-Share Index was higher 14 trading days later.

" there have been 22 years since 1970 when the UK market has either risen by more than 0.9 per cent or fallen by more than 0.5 per cent on Budget Day and the day after "

Reasons for the phenomenon

It is relatively easy to explain why share prices behave in this manner.

First, a very favourable reaction to the Budget from investors is likely to mean that sentiment will remain positive in the weeks after the Budget, which significantly increases the odds that share prices will rise in the subsequent 14-day trading period. Alternatively, if share prices have fallen too much following the Budget, then it is quite possible that investors have been too harsh in their initial reaction. In which case, there is scope for the market to bounce back, as it has done regularly in the past four decades.

trading strategy 36

Make the most of large moves post-Budget

If the UK market has either risen by more than 0.9 per cent or fallen by more than 0.5 per cent on Budget day and the day after, then it is worth becoming a buyer of the market for the next 14 trading days. Remember, in the past 4 decades, 90 per cent of the time when prices have traded in these ranges, the FTSE All-Share Index was higher 14 trading days later.

Mechanics of trading the UK market

The FTSE All-Share Index consists of the blue-chip FTSE 100, mid cap FTSE 250 and the FTSE small cap indices. The FTSE 100, however, has a weighting of over 75 per cent in the FTSE All-Share Index, so the two indices track each other very closely. Most investors prefer to trade the FTSE 100 instead of the FTSE All-Share as there are far more options for buying or selling it short.

Spread betting is one method for trading, where investors can place either an up bet (to buy) or down bet (to sell) for every point movement in the FTSE 100. Profits from spread betting are currently tax free in the UK. This trade is simple to execute and you can place a bet for as little as £1 per point movement on the FTSE 100. In the UK, spread betting firms include IG Index, City Index, Capital Spreads, CMC Markets and Cantor Index.

Another way to buy (but not sell) the FTSE 100 is through an ETF that tracks the performance of the Index, with each 1 per cent movement in the Index translating to a 1 per cent movement in the ETF. These include those issued by Lyxor (TIDM: L100), a subsidiary of French investment bank Société Générale, Deutsche Bank (TIDM: XUKX) and Barclays iShares (TIDM: ISF). ETFs can be bought or sold through stockbrokers in the same way as shares in any listed company.

chapter

18

Sporting chance

Without doubt, football is one of the most closely followed sports in the world and no more so than the FIFA World Cup, which takes place every four years. Outside North America, the tournament is probably one of the most prominent events in the sporting calendar, perhaps only coming second to the Olympic Games.

For instance, during the last World Cup in Germany in 2006, over 26 billion football fans in 214 countries viewed the event on television, including a staggering 715 million for the Italy versus France final.

That football has such a huge global audience is hardly a revelation. The fact that it has a direct and significant impact on the performance of the US stock market during the FIFA World Cup, though, probably is.

The FIFA World Cup and US equity returns

the FIFA World Cup has a direct and significant impact on the performance of the US stock market, the market falls, on average, by 2.58 per cent during the month-long tournament

Research by academics Guy Kaplanski and Haim Levy (2008) has proved just that. This may seem even more astounding because 'soccer', as Americans call football, is not very popular in the US, so, intuitively, you would expect that any impact from the tournament on its domestic stock market would, negative or positive, be minimal. That would be a bad mistake, however, as the study – which looked at the last 15 tournaments in the past 58 years – revealed that the US stock market falls, on average, by 2.58 per cent during the month-long tournament.

Reasons for the phenomenon

Without doubt, the US is the most important capital market in the world – so much so that transactions by non-US investors accounted for a hefty 33 per cent of all trades on the US stock market in 2006. This fact is important because, if the moods of overseas investors are affected by football results during the World Cup tournament – and specifically when their national teams lose a game – it could have a direct impact on how those investors behave in their day-to-day lives, including how they make investment decisions. In turn, given the large number of investors affected, this will have a direct impact on the US equity market.

> **" transactions by non-US investors accounted for a hefty 33 per cent of all trades on the US stock market in 2006, if the moods of overseas investors are affected by football results ... it could have a direct impact on how they make investment decisions "**

This is quite logical as we know that attitudes towards risk are affected by mood swings (see Chapters 3 and 5), so it is not a big leap to reason that our moods and our attitude to risk could be similarly affected by the outcomes of key football matches.

In their study, Kaplanski and Levy (2008) noted:

If there is a negative market effect driven by the losing country's investors, the change in the investment proportions (held) in risky and riskless assets is not just confined to the local stock market and we also expect a negative effect in the US market (given their presence in this market). Moreover, as the number of losing countries increases as the tournament progresses, we expect a cumulative large effect on the US stock market which may be even larger than the local market effect, despite the fact that soccer is not very popular in the US.

To explain how this negative effect impacts the US stock market in particular, the authors considered a game of football between England and Italy:

If England loses, British investors will sell (or not buy) stocks in the US market. If Italy loses, Italian investors will sell stocks in the US market. In both cases a negative effect in the US market does not depend on the game result.

The authors added:

As the tournament progresses, the number of fans experiencing disappointment – which for some involves sadness, stress and grief – also increases. Eventually, the majority of fans, comprising hundreds of millions of people, belong to a losing party and hence they are potential contributors to the global negative effect.

Kaplanski and Levy's theory is backed up by academics Alex Edmans, Diego Garcia and Oyvind Norli (2005). They proved that there is 'a significant negative stock market reaction to losses by national soccer teams.' This seems sensible as previous studies have shown that watching stressful soccer matches can affect our health and state of mind. For example, the incidence of heart attacks rose dramatically in Germany on days that the national soccer team were playing during the 2006 World Cup. Similarly, in the 3 days following England's loss against Argentina in the 1998 World Cup, heart-related emergencies at hospitals in England rose by 25 per cent.

> ❝ soccer events induce mood swings in the population, which may affect investors' behaviour and the willingness to take on risk, so affecting stock prices by the end of the football tournament ❞

Clearly, by the end of the tournament there are going to be more football fans and investors who have suffered disappointment and anxiety than elation, so there will be a negative net effect overall. As Kaplanski and Levy (2008) noted in their study:

Sports in general and soccer in particular play an immense role in many people's lives. This phenomenon may suggest that soccer events – especially the World Cup – induce mood swings in the population, which may affect investors' behaviour and the willingness to take on risk, so affecting stock prices.

Football fans are also affected by allegiance bias, whereby they are psychologically invested in a desired outcome. Edmans, Garcia and Oyvind (2005) found that, 'If the reference point of soccer fans is that their team will win, we may find a greater stock price reaction after losses than after wins.' This is important as, clearly, there can only be one winner of the tournament, so the total negative impact on the followers of all the 32 losing teams in the World Cup will be greater than any positive impact on the far smaller number of fans of the sole winner of the tournament. As Kaplanski and Levy (2008) neatly pointed out in their study, 'A loss hurts more than the joy derived from a gain of the same magnitude.'

> ❝ if the reference point of soccer is that their team will win, we may find a greater stock price reaction after losses than after wins ❞

The June and July effect

It is quite possible that, as the World Cup is a summer event, taking place in June and July, the poor investment returns in the US equity market are simply due to the US market performing poorly at this time of the year anyway. However, Kaplanski and Levy (2008) found in their study that there was no seasonal effect after analysing the performance of the stock market during the same months in years when the World Cup was *not* running.

> **" the natural way to exploit the tendency of the US stock market to perform poorly during the World Cup is to short sell the S&P 500 Index ... to try to profit from the average 2.58 per cent fall "**

In addition, they found that the returns from the stock market on trading days around the dates of the soccer matches were lower than the return for the whole of the relevant year. This indicates that, in good and bad years alike, there is a specific negative stock market effect related to the event itself.

trading strategy 37

Expoliting depression induced by World Cup losses

The natural way to exploit the tendency of the US stock market to perform poorly during the month-long FIFA World Cup is to short sell the S&P 500 Index shortly before the tournament starts and close this position after the final game has been played.

The easiest way to execute this trade to try to profit from the average 2.58 per cent fall in the Index throughout the tournament is through spread betting. Investors place a down bet for every point movement in the S&P 500. Although the Index is denominated in dollars, there is no foreign currency risk as the down bet can be placed in sterling for every point movement in the Index. Profits from spread betting are currently tax free in the UK. In the UK, spread betting firms include IG Index, City Index, Capital Spreads, CMC Markets and Cantor Index.

History lessons

etting against 100 years of stock market history can be very risky, especially if you know in advance the odds of the market rising or falling at certain points of the year. More importantly, there are specific reasons for these price trends having a habit of repeating themselves year in year out.

Trading Secrets reveals how you can position yourself to maximise profits and minimise potential losses by trading off this valuable knowledge and, in particular, avoid trading losses during the weakest-performing months of the year – May, June and September.

May day blues

Make no mistake, May has a terrible record. In fact, the UK stock market has produced a loss or around 0.5 per cent a year, on average, during this month for the past four decades, making it one of the weakest-performing months of the year.

> the six-month period from the start of May to the end of October is the worst time of the year to be invested in the stock market, with the FTSE All-Share Index rising by a pitiful 0.25 per cent since 1990

Moreover, we also know that the six-month period from the start of May to the end of October is the worst time of the year to be invested in the market, with the FTSE All-Share Index rising by a pitiful 0.25 per cent, on average, in this period since 1990.

By contrast, the period from the start of November to the end of April has recorded an average gain of 7.1 per cent for the past 17 years. That's reason enough to be cautious of being heavily invested in shares as we leave the seasonally strong six-month period at the end of April.

Reasons for the phenomenon

It's really not surprising that the market has a tendency to take a breather in May. For starters, the corporate reporting season timetable is heavily skewed towards companies with calendar year ends that report preliminary results in February and March, while those companies with March year ends will have already reported pre-close trading statements by the time we enter the month of May. Therefore, acting as it does as an efficient discounting mechanism, the market should have already factored in the good news from companies that have reported their financial results, as well as taken into account the trading statements from companies with March year ends that are due to report preliminary results from mid-May onwards.

❝ the rise in share prices during the first four months of the year is actually very logical ❞

In other words, the rise in share prices during the first four months of the year is actually very logical as we are getting a double whammy of news from companies both reporting results and those that are scheduled to report results from mid-May onwards. What this means, though, is that there is a greater possibility that most of the good news has been incorporated into share prices by the time we enter May, leaving scope for the market to perform poorly during the month.

Reading the warning signals

❝ in the past 5 decades, there have been 15 occasions when the FTSE All-Share Index has risen in the range of 2.9 per cent to 8.4 per cent during the month of April ❞

The key to trading through May is to avoid the pitfalls. Luckily, there are three major warning signals that enable us to take advantage of this month's poor record.

First, let's consider what happens when prices move up too quickly in April. That is a very bad omen for the performance of the market in May, which is hardly surprising considering that, the more the market rises in April, the more likely it is that all the good news has been factored into share prices by the start of May. In fact, in the past 5 decades, there have been 15 occasions when the FTSE All-Share Index has risen in the range of 2.9 per cent to 8.4 per cent during the month of April. In all bar one of those years, the stock market fell in May.

This trend was originally uncovered by stock market historian David Schwartz over a decade ago, which I have subsequently updated (Thompson, 2008b). The one exception to the rule was in 2003, when the UK market rose by 6.3 per cent in April and 4.1 per cent in May, albeit this marked the beginning of the 2003–2007 bull market. The 5.9 per cent rise in the FTSE All-Share Index in April 2008 made it number 16 in the series. Again, prices fell in May (by 0.6 per cent), maintaining this amazing track record.

> **❝❝ there have only been 11 years when the UK market fell in the range of 5.3 to 12.7 per cent between the start of January and end of April ❞❞**

A second warning signal should be flashing when there have been pretty savage declines in share prices in the first four months of the year. Again, I can thank Mr Schwartz for pointing me in the right direction on this. Going back over the past 8 decades, there have only been 11 years when the UK market fell in the range of 5.3 to 12.7 per cent between the start of January and end of April (Thompson, 2008b). In no fewer than 9 of those 11 years, the market continued to fall in May, including 6 occasions when the UK stock market declined by more than 5 per cent during the month. The two exceptions were in 2000 (when the FTSE All-Share Index fell by 7.4 per cent in the first 4 months of the year, but managed to edge up 0.5 per cent during May) and in 1973 (when the return in May was barely in profit).

> **❝❝ over 80 years of history suggests that the odds are heavily stacked against the UK market making headway during the month of May if it has already sustained heavy falls during the preceding 4 months ❞❞**

In other words, over 80 years of history suggests that the odds are heavily stacked against the UK market making headway during the month of May if it has already sustained heavy falls during the preceding 4 months. This is hardly surprising as falls of that nature increase the odds that a bear market is in progress. With this thought in mind, it's worth noting that the FTSE All-Share Index fell by 5.68 per cent between the start of January and the end of April 2008, making it number 12 in the series. True to form, share prices in May 2008 fell again, with the Index down by 0.6 per cent for the month.

Confirming the theory that the good news is already factored into share prices by the time we reach May, Mr Schwartz (2008d) has uncovered

> ❝ if the market has run up too strongly in April, this clearly increases the odds of a down month in May ❞

another trend that has become very common in recent years: the market has a tendency to fall between 7 May and 26 May. In fact, in the past decade, the FTSE 100 index has fallen no fewer than nine times between these two dates. Interestingly, 2008 was no exception, with share prices plunging by over 2 per cent in this period (see Table 19.1).

table 19.1 FTSE 100 Index price changes between 7 and 26 May, 1998–2008

Year	Index at close on 6 May	Index at close on 26 May	Percentage change (%)
1998	5987	5969	−0.3
1999	6401	6236	−2.6
2000	6238	6231	−0.1
2001	5765	5916	2.6
2002	5203	5169	−0.7
2003	4006	3980	−0.6
2004	4516	4438	−1.7
2005	4918	4995	1.6
2006	6091	5791	−4.9
2007	6603	6570	−0.5
2008	6215	6087	−2.1

Source: Thomson Reuters Datastream

trading strategy 38

Profit from the May day blues

If the market has run up too strongly in April, this clearly increases the odds of a down month in May. We can profit from this, but to maximise gains, it is probably best to wait to short sell the FTSE 100 after 6 May to take advantage of expected profit-taking by investors as the prior run-up in share prices has a habit of continuing into the first week of May before peaking out. This strategy also takes advantage of the trend for the market to fall between 7 and 26 May.

One way to execute this trade is through a spread bet. Short selling the market is when you place a down spread bet on the FTSE 100, so this trade makes a profit when the Index falls in value, but a loss if it rises. The easiest way to do this is through a spread betting firm. The trade is simple to execute and you can place a bet for as little as £1 per point movement on the FTSE 100. In the UK, spread betting firms include IG Index, City Index, Capital Spreads, CMC Markets and Cantor Index.

trading strategy 39

Another way to beat the May day blues

This second low-risk trading strategy is to short sell the FTSE 100 through a spread bet during May when prices have moved too high above their end of April close, but only if the market has already sustained heavy losses in the first four months of the year. As eight decades of history proves, the chances of the market rising in May are very slim indeed if it has already fallen heavily during the year to date.

In fact, the UK stock market has never managed to rise more than 0.5 per cent in May if it has sustained painful losses during the previous four months. This is hardly surprising as falls of that nature increase the odds that a bear market is in progress. In fact, the chances that the market will rise during May in a bear market are roughly only one in four.

❝ the UK stock market has never managed to rise more than 0.5 per cent in May if it has sustained painful losses during the previous four months ❞

June stock market showers

Investors hoping to get some respite from their May blues are unlikely to find trading conditions in June any better. It is one of the weakest months of the year, with the FTSE 100 posting an average loss of 0.8 per cent in the past 4 decades. There is less than a 50:50 chance of making a profit by being invested in the FTSE 100 during this month.

Reasons for the phenomenon

The problem is that, every five or six years, the market has a nasty tendency to fall significantly during the month. Given that similar price falls are seen in May every five years or so as well, it makes this two-month period one of the most treacherous for equity market investors. Moreover, because the market only rises a minuscule 0.5 per cent, on

❝ because the market only rises a miniscule 0.5 per cent, on average, in a good June during bull market years, investors are hardly getting adequate compensation to offset the regular heavy hits received during one of the much more frequent bad Junes ❞

average, in a good June during bull market years, investors are hardly getting adequate compensation to offset the regular heavy hits received during one of the much more frequent bad Junes.

True, the market did rise during June in the bull market years of 2004, 2005 and 2006, but it's worth noting that it also posted modest losses in the bull market years of 2007 and 2003 (see Table 19.2).

Remember, seasonal investing rules apply and, in the past two decades, it has been very difficult to show a profit for the six-month period from the end of April to the end of October. There may be some merit in the folklore that the top dogs in the City are more interested in the sporting season – Ascot, Henley and test match cricket at Lords – than playing the financial markets at this time of the year.

❝ remember, seasonal investing rules apply and, in the past two decades, it has been very difficult to show a profit for the six-month period from the end of April to the end of October ❞

June definitely stands out when bear markets are in progress, with prices falling in the month around 90 per cent of the time. True to form, the FTSE 100 fell heavily during the month in both 2001 and 2002, during the savage 2000–2003 bear market, and 2008 was no different – the Index plunging by over 7 per cent during the month (see Table 19.2) in the midst of the bear market that started in the autumn of 2007.

trading strategy 40

Short sell the FTSE 100 at the end of May

A warning signal should be flashing red as we enter June if a bear market is running as there is a 90 per cent chance the market will fall during the month, with roughly a one in two chance that the decline will be significant. This is your cue to short sell the FTSE 100 through a spread bet at the end of May, especially if the Index has fallen in the second half of the month as the downward momentum has a habit of continuing into June, especially during bear markets.

table 19.2 FTSE 100 Index price changes between 31 May and 30 June, 1998–2008

Year	Index close on 31 May	Index close on 30 June	Percentage change (%)
1998	5865	5866	0.0
1999	6226	6318	1.5
2000	6359	6312	−0.7
2001	5796	5642	−2.7
2002	5040	4632	−8.1
2003	4048	4031	−0.4
2004	4430	4512	1.9
2005	4964	5109	2.9
2006	5723	5833	1.9
2007	6621	6607	−0.2
2008	6053	5625	−7.1

Source: Thomson Reuters Datastream

> ❝ a warning signal should be flashing red as we enter June if a bear market is running as there is a 90 per cent chance the market will fall during the month ❞

September can be chilly

It's not only in May and June that the performance of the market sends shivers down the spines of investors and wreaks havoc with portfolios. September has a truly appalling record, too, with the UK stock market falling by 1.3 per cent, on average, during the month in the past 4 decades. Moreover, the second week in September has the worst performance record for any week of the year, while the fourth week is not far behind it.

Reasons for the phenomenon

> ❝ part of the reason for September registering some pretty horrific market falls lies with the US: it is the worst month of the year on Wall Street ❞

Part of the reason for September registering some pretty horrific market falls lies with the US: it is the worst month of the year on Wall Street. In fact, the Dow Jones Industrial Average has only risen 22 times during September in the past 6 decades, posting an average loss of 0.9 per cent. That impacts UK investors directly because of the relatively close relationship in price movements of the two stock markets.

For instance, between 1998 and 2003, the FTSE 100 fell in September every single year, including some eye-watering hits during the bear market of

❝ in the past four decades, a bear market has been running during September on eight occasions, the market fell in every one of these months ❞

2000–2003 (see Table 19.3). In 2001, prices were hammered by the 9/11 terrorist attacks in New York and, in 2002, the market was spooked by the prospect of an imminent war in Iraq. Even during the end of the 1990s bull market, the Index still registered some nasty losses of 3.5 per cent in both 1998 and 1999. What's more, September is particularly bad during bear markets. In the past four decades, a bear market has been running during

September on nine occasions. The market fell in every one of these months, with share prices dropping by over 5 per cent each time, including a 13 per cent drop in September 2008.

table 19.3 FTSE 100 Index price changes between 1 and 30 September, 1998–2008

Year	Index close on 31 August	Index close on 30 September	Percentage change (%)
1998	5249	5064	−3.5
1999	6246	6030	−3.5
2000	6672	6294	−5.7
2001	5345	4903	−8.3
2002	4227	3721	−12.0
2003	4161	4091	−1.7
2004	4459	4588	2.9
2005	5296	5478	3.4
2006	5906	5960	0.9
2007	6303	6466	2.6
2008	5637	4902	−13.0

Source: Thomson Reuters Datastream

trading strategy 41

Short sell the FTSE 100 at the start of September

If a bear market is running, then you can confidently short sell the FTSE 100 through a down spread bet at the start of September.

In recent years, investors following this strategy will have made significant gains, as the market fell heavily in September in 2000, 2001, 2002 and 2008. In fact, this trade has a 100 per cent track record spanning four decades, with nine profitable shorting months and no losses.

Equally, if a bull market is running, the chances of sustaining a nasty hit during the month of September is much reduced. For instance, when the FTSE 100 posted solid rises in August in 2004, 2005 and 2007 during the 2003–2007 bull market (see Table 19.4), the Index continued to rise strongly during September (see Table 19.3). Therefore, do not attempt to short sell the FTSE 100 at the end of August if a bull market is running and if the market has posted a significant rise during the month as the odds of the price momentum running through into September increase greatly. Still, even if August has produced a positive return, it is simply too risky to try and buck September's appalling record and try to make money by buying the FTSE 100 at the start of the month. September is very much a month for the bears.

❝ even if August has produced a positive return, it is simply too risky to try and buck September's appalling record ❞

table 19.4 FTSE 100 Index price changes between 31 July and 31 August, 1998–2008

Year	Index close on 31 July	Index close on 31 August	Percentage change (%)
1998	5827	5249	−9.9
1999	6231	6246	0.2
2000	6365	6672	4.8
2001	5529	5345	−3.3
2002	4246	4227	−0.4
2003	4157	4161	0.1
2004	4418	4459	0.9
2005	5282	5296	0.3
2006	5928	5906	−0.4
2007	6206	6303	1.6
2008	5412	5636	4.1

Source: Thomson Reuters Datastream

20

Triple witching effect

'Triple witching' may sound like something that has more in common with Hallowe'en than the financial markets. Investors ignore these important dates on the calendar at their peril, though, as they have a significant impact on how the equity markets behave at certain points of the year.

> **"** investors ignore these important dates on the calendar at their peril as Triple Witching has a significant impact on how the equity markets behave **"**

Futures, options and triple witching

Most investors have a portfolio of shares and ETFs that track the performance of an index such as the FTSE 100 or an individual sector of the stock market. However, very experienced traders and financial institutions also use derivative products, such as options and futures contracts, that track the movements of the underlying shares and indices. These products enable investors to increase the amount of gearing they get relative to movements in the underlying assets, so increasing the potential to make greater profits. Some of those options and future contracts can be highly geared, moving sometimes 20 to 30 times more than the underlying asset.

This sophisticated option and futures market is very large and traded through the London International Financial Futures Exchange, commonly known as the Liffe. The contracts – which are specifically stock options, stock index futures and stock futures – have set dates for expiry and are settled on those dates throughout the year. On four dates every three months, however – the third Friday of March, June, September and December – all three of the derivative contracts have the same expiry date, hence the name 'triple witching'. These are important dates to remember because traders who hold such options and futures contracts clearly have a vested interest in making sure that the price of the underlying share or index traded on the London Stock Exchange is moving in their favour when settlement of their Liffe contracts takes place.

For instance, if a trader holds call options in BP, giving him or her the right to buy shares in the company at a specific predetermined price when the option contract is settled, then, the higher the BP price is at the close of trading on the Friday when settlement occurs, the more profit the trader will make. If you consider that hundreds of similar contracts are all being settled at the same time, you can see how this can give rise to some very strange price movements in both shares of these FTSE 100 companies and also in the Index itself.

That is because some traders will try to force up the share prices of companies like BP at the time of the settlement of their Liffe options and futures contracts so that they maximise the profit on those contracts. Similarly, some traders may try to force down the share prices of companies in which they own put options (these give the holder of the option the right to sell shares in the company at a predetermined price when the option contract is settled). To complicate matters even further, triple witching also occurs on these same four days in the US stock market.

> **most investors will not really know why these blue-chip shares are moving in such an odd fashion and may end up losing money**

The frenetic trading in these options and futures contracts – as well as in the underlying shares on which the contracts settlement price is based – gives rise to much higher volatility in share prices on these settlement days than usual. It also greatly influences the closing prices of shares at the end of trading on those Fridays by creating unusual buying and selling pressure on the share prices of some of the FTSE 100 companies. Most investors will not really know why these blue-chip shares are moving in such an odd fashion and may end up losing money as a result. By following a few simple rules, however, we can take advantage of these price swings and make money from trading the FTSE 100 in the week after these options and futures contracts expire.

Trading triple witching: March settlement

March is a good time to be invested in the stock market as it is in the seasonally strong November through to April period for investing (see Chapter 5). Moreover, we know that the US stock market has a habit of getting a boost around the time of St Patrick's day, which falls on 17 March each year, as well as in triple witching week (see Chapter 14).

As the US market and the UK market are highly correlated, so have a tendency to move in the same direction, then positive share price movements on Wall Street are generally good news for the UK stock market.

It therefore pays to know when the month is likely to fail to give its customary boost to the value of your shareholdings. Fortunately, a trend has developed specifically related to triple witching that gives us the edge.

In the past decade, when the FTSE 100 has fallen heavily (by 1 per cent or more) in the week before TWW in March, it has been a bad omen for

table 20.1 Performance of FTSE 100 Index before, during and after triple witching week in March

Year	Percentage return before expiration week	Percentage return during expiration week	Percentage return week after
1998	−0.03	3.11	−0.47
1999	1.24	−1.89	−0.39
2000	1.25	−0.15	2.75
2001	1.01	−6.00	0.25
2002	2.22	0.13	−0.80
2003	3.15	7.22	−3.97
2004	−1.75	−1.12	−1.35
2005	−1.07	−1.18	0.00
2006	0.83	1.56	0.61
2007	2.11	−1.85	3.40
2008	−1.19	−2.42	3.58
Average	0.71	−0.12	−0.12
Up	7	4	6
Down	4	7	5

Source: Thomson Reuters Datastream

> a trend has developed specifically related to triple witching that gives us the edge ... when the FTSE 100 has fallen heavily the week before triple witching week it has been a bad omen for the performance of the market the following week

the performance of the market the following week (see Table 20.1). In 2004, a 1.75 per cent fall in the market the week before TWW was followed by a 1.12 per cent decline during options week. It was a similar story in 2005 when a 1.07 per cent fall in the FTSE 100 the week before TWW was followed by a 1.18 per cent decline the week after. And the trend is holding up well, with the FTSE 100 falling by 1.19 per cent and 2.42 per cent, respectively, in these two weeks in 2008.

Reasons for the phenomenon

When the stock market fails to make headway during a seasonally good time for investing, and in particular in the run-up to options expiry week when traders are positioning themselves to maximise profits on options and futures contracts, then it is a clear signal of general weakness in prices, in the short term at least. In turn, this weakness could easily spill over into TWW when those contracts are settled. That has certainly been the case for the past decade and it's clearly worth taking note when this happens.

trading strategy 42

TWW in March

The market is sending a clear short-term trading signal when its performance in the week before TWW is poor. So, if the FTSE 100 has fallen by at least 1 per cent in that week, look to profit from the expected fall in share prices the week after by short selling the Index just before the market closes on the Friday before TWW. That strategy has proved very profitable in the past decade.

The trading strategy is to keep this short index trade open until close of trading on the Friday of TWW, although, clearly, if you are sitting on significant paper profits, then banking some of those gains early is never a bad move.

The easiest way to execute this trade is to place a down spread bet on the FTSE 100 through a spread betting firm. In the UK, these include companies such as City Index, IG Index, Capital Spreads, Cantor Index and CMC Markets. Profits from spread betting are currently tax free in the UK and you can place a bet from as little as £1 per point movement in the Index.

Trading triple witching: June settlement

June is a wretched month for investing (see Chapter 19). In fact, in bear markets, there is a 90 per cent chance the market will fall during the

❝ in bear markets, there is a 90 per cent chance that the stock market will fall during the month ❞

month, with roughly a one in two chance that the decline will be significant. Even if we are in a bull market, the average gain of 0.5 per cent recorded during those months is hardly adequate compensation, given the risk of encountering a poor bull market month.

This helps explain why the market has only risen 4 times in the past 11 years in the week before TWW in June and just 6 times in TWW itself. Moreover, when the market takes a nasty hit in TWW with the FTSE 100 falling by 3 per cent or more, as has happened twice in this 11-year period, it has never once risen the following week (see Table 20.2). For instance, the FTSE 100 fell by 3.13 per cent in TWW in 2008 and followed this with a 1.63 per cent decline the week after. It was a similar story in 2001, with a hefty 3.82 per cent fall in TWW followed by a 1.01 loss in the subsequent five trading days.

table 20.2 Performance of FTSE 100 Index before, during and after TWW in June

Year	Percentage return before expiration week	Percentage return during expiration week	Percentage return week after
1998	−3.00	−0.26	2.12
1999	1.93	0.66	−1.41
2000	−2.76	1.29	−2.07
2001	2.43	−3.82	−1.01
2002	−5.90	−0.54	0.58
2003	−0.39	0.63	−2.53
2004	0.67	0.46	−0.25
2005	0.62	0.94	0.03
2006	−2.00	−1.02	1.70
2007	−2.57	3.48	−2.46
2008	−1.77	−3.13	−1.63
Average	**−1.16**	**−0.12**	**−0.63**
Up	4	6	4
Down	7	5	7

Source: Thomson Reuters Datastream

trading strategy 43

Profit from the TWW in June

If the FTSE 100 has fallen by 3 per cent or more in TWW, it increases the odds significantly that a bear market is running. Look to profit from the expected fall in share prices the week after by short selling the Index, placing a spread down bet just before the market closes on the Friday of TWW. The strategy is to keep that short index trade open until close of trading on the Friday after TWW. It has shown a profit every time in the past decade.

Reasons for the phenomenon

June falls in the seasonally weak May to October period for investing (see Chapter 5). So, the fact that, on average, the FTSE 100 struggles to make any headway in both TWW and the weeks before and after is understandable. The market, however, is sending out a distress signal that all is not well when hefty falls of 3 per cent plus are recorded in TWW. More market participants and short-term traders are clearly net sellers and not buyers, which should be heeded. Moreover, hefty falls in the FTSE 100 in June are commonplace in bear markets. As the market has fallen in June around 90 per cent of the time during bear markets, then it really is not surprising that large losses during TWW are followed by a poor performance the week after.

> **❝ hefty falls in the FTSE 100 in June are commonplace in bear markets ❞**

Trading triple witching: September settlement

> **❝ if June is a bad month for investing, then September is an absolute shocker, with the FTSE 100 Index falling, on average, by 1.3 per cent during the month for the past 4 decades ❞**

If June is a bad month for investing, then September is an absolute shocker, with the FTSE 100 Index falling, on average, by 1.3 per cent during the month for the past 4 decades. Moreover, the second week of June – which generally falls the week before TWW – is historically the worst week of the year. In fact, in the past 11 years the Index has fallen no fewer than 8 times the week before TWW.

So if prices fall heavily the week before TWW, by 1 per cent or more, this is the signal to aggressively short sell the Index through a spread bet during TWW. In the past decade when the FTSE 100 has fallen by 1 per cent or more the week before TWW it has continued to fall the following week on every occasion, including some eye-watering losses in every year between 1998 and 2002 (see Table 20.3).

Reasons for the phenomenon

Part of the reason for the UK stock market registering some pretty horrific market falls in September lies with the US stock market as the month is

❝ the Dow Jones Industrial Average has only risen 22 times during September in the past 6 decades, posting an average loss of 0.9 per cent ❞

by far the worst of the year on Wall Street. In fact, the Dow Jones Industrial Average has only risen 22 times during September in the past 6 decades, posting an average loss of 0.9 per cent. This impacts the UK market directly, given the close relationship between price moves on the FTSE 100 and Wall Street.

table 20.3 Performance of FTSE 100 Index before, during and after TWW in September

Year	Percentage return before expiration week	Percentage return during expiration week	Percentage return week after
1998	−0.95	−1.23	0.11
1999	−2.22	−2.46	−1.69
2000	−2.86	−2.78	−3.29
2001	−6.21	−6.78	10.59
2002	−2.41	−3.69	1.22
2003	−0.46	0.45	−2.34
2004	−0.05	1.01	−0.28
2005	0.61	0.90	0.01
2006	−1.18	−0.03	−0.93
2007	1.58	2.65	0.02
2008	3.35	−1.94	−4.20
Average	−0.98	−1.17	−0.07
Up	3	4	5
Down	8	7	6

Source: Thomson Reuters Datastream

trading strategy 44

Profit from the TWW in September

If the FTSE 100 falls by one per cent or more in the week before TWW, look to profit from the expected fall in share prices the week after by short selling the Index through a spread down bet just before the market closes on the Friday before the start of TWW. The strategy is to keep this short Index trade open until close of trading on the Friday of TWW. This trading strategy has a 100 per cent track record – every one of the five trades has been profitable in the past 11 years – with the average gain on these trades around 3.15 per cent, the equivalent of 157 points on the FTSE 100.

Trading triple witching: December settlement

December is the best month to be invested in equities and I have previously noted that the period between 11 December and 5 January is the ideal time to be invested in the market (see Chapter 10). This trade has shown a generous 2.5 per cent profit, on average, for the past 28 years, with a 85 per cent success rate.

❝❝ between 11 December and 5 January is the ideal time to be invested in the market ❞❞

The performance of the market in December has been generally poor in the week before TWW (the second week of the month) with the FTSE 100 falling in all bar two of the past 10 years. The good news is that these falls set the market up for some bumper gains during TWW and the week after. In fact, buying the FTSE 100 just before the close of trading on the Friday before TWW, and holding this position for the following two weeks, has reaped bumper profits over the past decade. The trade has shown an average profit of 1.30 per cent over the two week period, posting eight out of ten winning trades.

This is understandable as the softness in stock prices in the first 11 days of December sets the market up nicely for a bounce back in TWW. This positive momentum more often than not continues into the fourth week of December which coincides with the period around Christmas – historically some of the best days of the year to be invested in the market (see Chapter 10).

table 20.4 Performance of FTSE 100 Index before, during and after TWW in December

Year	Percentage return before expiration week	Percentage return during expiration week	Percentage return week after
1998	−0.71	3.61	2.20
1999	−0.04	−0.24	1.22
2000	1.91	−1.80	−1.27
2001	−3.86	1.93	1.61
2002	−3.37	0.28	−1.54
2003	−0.46	1.50	0.73
2004	−1.11	0.06	1.42
2005	−0.19	0.25	1.16
2006	2.18	1.76	−1.11
2007	−2.41	0.58	0.65
Average	**−0.81**	**0.79**	**0.51**
Up	2	8	7
Down	8	2	3

Source: Thomson Reuters Datastream

Reasons for the phenomenon

It is a common to see trading volumes tail off in the run-up to Christmas as dealers and City professionals shut up shop for the festive period. As a result of this, liquidity starts to dry up and, given that the only market participants still trading are likely to be buyers of stocks, then, in the absence of sellers, we have conditions that are ripe for the market to rise on very low volumes in the final week of the year. Also, as TWW, the third week of the month, falls in the period between Friday 15 December and Friday 21 December, it also overlaps with some of those profitable trading days around Christmas.

trading strategy 45

Profit from the TWW in December

If you are not already invested in the market by 11 December, the optimum trade is to take advantage of the FTSE 100's tendency to rise in the run-up to Christmas and the days around this festive holiday by buying the Index through a spread up bet at the close of trading on the Friday before TWW. Look to take profits on this trade around 5 January to make the most of the expected rise in the market during TWW and in the period around Christmas and the New Year.

References

Arnold, Glen and Baker, Rose (2007) 'Return reversal in UK shares', Centre for Economic and Finance Research, Salford Business School, University of Salford.

Bohl, Martin and Salm, Christian (2007) 'The other January effect: nothing more than a statistical artifact', Westfalische Wilhelms-University, Munster.

Cooper, Michael, McConnell, John and Ovtchinnikov, Alexai (2006) 'The other January effect', *Journal of Financial Economics*, November.

Coutts, Andrew (1999) 'Friday the thirteenth and the Financial Times Industrial Ordinary Shares Index 1935–1994', *Applied Economics Letters*.

Dahya, Jay (2006) 'Playing footsie with the FTSE 100', City University of New York, 11 January.

De Bondt, Werner F.M. and Thaler, Richard H. (1987) 'Further evidence on investor overreaction and stock market seasonality', *The Journal of Finance*, 42 (3): 557–81.

Dillow, Chris (2007) 'Do sectors overreact?', *Investors Chronicle*, 14 November.

Edmans, Alex, Garcia, Diego and Norli, Oyvind (2005) 'Sports sentiment and stock returns', EFA 2005 Moscow Meetings, Sixteenth Annual Utah Winter Finance Conference.

Frieder, Laura and Subrahmanyam, Avanidhar (2003) 'Testing for non-secular regularities in stock returns and trading activity', The Anderson School of Management, University of California.

Green, Kirsty (2007) 'Bringing home the bacon', Investors Chronicle, 7 February.

Hester, William (2007) 'Must stocks rise following a cut in the Federal Reserve funds rate', Hussman Funds, March. Available at: www.hussmanfunds.net

Hussman, John (2007) 'Market intervals go negative', Hussman Funds, 30 July. Available at: www.hussmanfunds.net

Kamstra, Mark, Kramer, Lisa and Levi, Maurice (2000) 'Losing sleep in the market: the daylight saving anomaly', *American Financial Review*, September.

Kamstra, Mark, Kramer, Lisa and Levi, Maurice (2003) 'Winter blues: a SAD stock market cycle', *The American Economic Review*, March.

Kaplanski, Guy and Levy, Haim (2008) 'Exploitable predictable irrationality: the FIFA World Cup effect on US stock market', May.

Lucey, Brian (2002) 'Friday the 13th & the philosophical basis of financial economics', *Journal of Economics and Finance*, 24 (3): 294–301.

Mase, Brian (2007) 'The impact of changes to the FTSE 100 Index', *The Financial Review*, August.

Mills, Terence and Coutts, Andrew (1995) 'Calendar effects in the London Stock Exchange FTSE indices', *The European Journal of Finance*.

Murphy, Paul (2008) 'Bear or super bear? The new Draaisma-land', *FT Alphaville*, 27 May.

Nickles, Dr Marshall (2004) 'Presidential elections and stock market cycles', Pepperdine University's Graziadio School of Business and Management.

Picarda, Dominic (2008) 'Bearing up', *Investors Chronicle*, 8 February.

Reynolds, Alan (2008) 'Why I am not using the R-word', *Financial Times*, 3 January.

Schwartz, David (2006a) 'The January rule: some sense much nonsense', London Stock Exchange, February.

Schwartz, David (2006b) 'Good trading prospects often surround Budget day', London Stock Exchange, March.

Schwartz, David (2006c) 'Big May–June declines send a worrying signal', London Stock Exchange, July.

Schwartz, David (2006d) 'Channel your trading strategy with trading channels', London Stock Exchange, 28 July.

Schwartz, David (2007a) 'Poor stock market conditions likely to continue', London Stock Exchange, 16 August.

Schwartz, David (2007b) 'Volatility is a bear market signal', London Stock Exchange, 6 December.

Schwartz, David (2008a) 'Fresh facts about the bear market of 2007–8', London Stock Exchange.

Schwartz, David (2008b) 'The bull market cupboard is bare', London Stock Exchange, 4 January.

Schwartz, David (2008c) 'History warns this bear market has further to run', London Stock Exchange, 17 March.

Schwartz, David (2008d) 'May be or may be not this May', *Financial Times*, 10 May.

Sonders, Liz Ann (2008) 'Fight the Fed sometimes', Charles Schwab Stockbrokers, 24 March.

Stack, James (2007) 'Bear market warning flags', *Forbes.com*, 27 July.

Thompson, Simon (1999) 'How to beat the FTSE 100', *Investors Chronicle*, 20 August.

Thompson, Simon (2005a) 'Playing footsie with the laggards', *Investors Chronicle*, 22 April.

Thompson, Simon (2005b) 'My sweet sixteen', *Investors Chronicle*, 16 November.

Thompson, Simon (2006) 'Playing footsie', *Investors Chronicle*, 24 November.

Thompson, Simon (2007a) 'Time to take stock', *Investors Chronicle*, 15 February.

Thompson, Simon (2007b) 'The party's over', *Investors Chronicle*, 25 June.

Thompson, Simon (2007c) 'Dow theory', *Investors Chronicle*, 9 July.

Thompson, Simon (2007d) 'Dow theory – Part Two', *Investors Chronicle*, 13 August.

Thompson, Simon (2007e) 'Investing through the credit squeeze', London Stock Exchange Market Programme, 24 August.

Thompson, Simon (2008a) 'Histrionics', *Investors Chronicle*, 7 April.

Thompson, Simon (2008b) 'Probability theory', *Investors Chronicle*, 16 May.

Thompson, Simon (2008b) 'Goodbye Mr Bond', *Investors Chronicle*, 4 July.

Thompson, Simon (2008c) 'The anatomy of the bear', *Investors Chronicle*, 7 July.

Thompson, Simon (2008d) 'Bear market rally for bulls', *Investors Chronicle*, 21 July.

Thompson, Simon and Dillow, Chris (2003) 'One step plan', *Investors Chronicle*, 3 October.

Wagner, Hans (2007) 'Stock market returns after rate cuts', Financial Sense University, 24 September.

Index

US bull markets *see* bull markets
US Central Bank *see* Federal Reserve
US consumer confidence as indicator,
    12
US dollar, effect of weakness, 15, 29
US presidential cycle, 71–84
    and bear market bottoms, 19, 77, 80
    and fiscal and monetary policy, 72–3
    and UK stock market, 73–81
    as indicator, 6–7, 18
    impact on US stock market, 73–81
    strategies to exploit, 76, 77–8, 80–1
    versus UK electoral process, 71
US recessions
    and bull market tops, 8–10
    and UK bear markets, 14
US yield curve and buy-on-second
    rate-cut strategy, 67–9

value stocks, 45
volatility index (VIX), 2
    as indicator of bottom, 20–1
    as indicator of top, 2–4
volatility and triple witching, 161
volatility risk of dog stocks, 129

weighting of US indices, 4
window dressing by fund managers, 98,
    128, 130
World Cup *see* FIFA World Cup

Yom Kippur (Day of Atonement),
    104–7, 108
    future dates of, 107
    strategy to exploit, 107, 108

Simon Thompson's Trading Strategies

READ INVESTORS CHRONICLE
FOR MORE TRADING SECRETS...

INVESTORS CHRONICLE

PROFIT TIPS AND FEATURES FOR PRIVATE INVESTORS

To subscribe now and save up to £47 off the cover price* call 0844 848 0106, quoting reference "ts" or visit www.investorschronicle.co.uk/ts to subscribe online.

*Saving based on the difference between buying 51 issues at the newsstand at £3.60 per issue (£183.60 in total) and subscribing by Direct Debit for 51 issues at £136. The cost of subscribing by credit card is £146 for 51 issues. Offer for new subscribers only. Offer closes 31.10.2010. Offer is for subscribers in the UK only. Please visit www.investorschronicle.co.uk for overseas subscription rates or to subscribe to our online service IC Advantage.